The Governance of Inclusive Growth

Please cite this publication as:
OECD (2016), *The Governance of Inclusive Growth*, OECD Publishing, Paris.
http://dx.doi.org/10.1787/9789264257993-en

ISBN 978-92-64-25798-6 (print)
ISBN 978-92-64-25799-3 (PDF)

Photo credits: Cover © Tomas Nihlén and A plus M Design.

Corrigenda to OECD publications may be found on line at: *www.oecd.org/about/publishing/corrigenda.htm.*

Foreword

Inclusive growth, or economic growth that benefits all by providing greater opportunity and sharing the fruits of prosperity evenly across society, is the subject of many policy and political discussions today. Recently, efforts have been made to broaden the discussion of growth and inequality beyond income to take into account a variety of outcomes across dimensions that affect people's well-being, such as jobs and health. To complement these policy discussions, it is necessary to look at the public governance of inclusive growth, with emphasis on the conditions that support not only the design, but also the implementation and evaluation, of policies for inclusive growth.

This report suggests an integrated approach to public governance for inclusive growth that relies not only on robust, aligned policy-making tools and processes, but also a "policy-shaping" environment grounded in openness, accountability and engagement with stakeholders.

Improving coherence and co-ordination across policy areas and levels of government can help governments identify where and how policies can complement and reinforce each other in pursuit of inclusive growth. In many countries, fragmented systems of governance hinder inclusiveness, leading to avoidable policy trade-offs and co-ordination failures. Public sector tools and processes, including steering, resource allocation and evaluation mechanisms, can be strengthened and aligned across the policy cycle to enable the pursuit of a whole-of-government vision for inclusive growth. New approaches to service delivery can be further pursued to improve the quality and reach of essential services, thus better connecting people with opportunity.

Moreover, the political and institutional structures that govern the economy need to ensure they represent and serve all segments of society. Open government and public engagement in policy making and service delivery can contribute to this while ensuring more effective policies and services. A policy-making process that is informed, inclusive and designed to aggregate competing interests helps ensure that inclusiveness and well-being are at the core of economic policies.

This report informed the discussion among ministers responsible for public sector reform at the Public Governance Ministerial Meeting held in Helsinki, Finland in October 2015. It will also contribute to and inform future OECD work on governance for inclusive growth, by providing a necessary focus on the "how" of policy making for inclusive growth and its political economy implications.

ACKNOWLEDGEMENTS

This report is the result of a collective effort from the Public Governance and Territorial Development Directorate (GOV), which is headed by Rolf Alter, Director, and Luiz de Mello, Deputy Director. Paloma Baena Olabe led a team of experts in the development and support of the report, they included: Julio Bacio Terracino, Monica Brezzi, Ronnie Downes, Céline Kaufmann and Tatyana Teplova.

The report was drafted by: Paloma Baena Olabe (Chapter 1), who also provided the overall editorial leadership; Ronnie Downes (Chapter 2); and Céline Kaufmann (Chapter 3). Major drafting contributions were received from Monica Brezzi, Barbara Ubaldi, Daniel Gerson, Julio Bacio Terracino, Aziza Akhmouch, Alessandro Bellantoni, Daniel Trnka, Marco Daglio, Tatyana Teplova and Stéphane Jacobzone.

Special thanks goes to Bill Below, Andrea Uhrhammer, Lynda Hawe, Anne Wojciechowski, Catherine Roch and Kate Lancaster for their help in preparing the report for publication.

Table of contents

Executive summary **9**

Chapter 1. **Pursuing inclusive growth: The Governance Underpinnings** **11**

A shift towards inclusive growth 12
The OECD work on inclusive growth 15
The governance underpinnings of inclusive growth 15
Policy making for inclusive growth: an integrated governance approach 18
Pursuing inclusive growth: The governance underpinnings 21
Notes 22
References 25

Chapter 2. **Policy making for inclusive growth: aligning design, delivery and accountability** **27**

Towards a strategic policy cycle 28
The case for a whole-of-government approach: Fostering co-ordination and the role of centres of government 31
Building a shared vision 32
Managing trade-offs and shaping actions for impact 37
Promoting government accountability for inclusive growth 45
Making service delivery more inclusive 47
Closing the policy cycle: evaluation, accountability and learning 53
Towards better policy making for inclusive growth 56
Notes 58
References 60

Chapter 3. **Shaping policies for inclusive growth: voice, inclusion and engagement** **63**

Shaping outcomes that matter most 64
Engaging stakeholders and preventing capture: Inclusive policy making through stakeholder engagement 65
Shaping vision and delivery through stakeholder engagement 69
Leveraging tools for engagement, from information to co-creation 72
Addressing the challenge of engagement 80
Shaping better outcomes through an inclusive public sector workforce 86
Mainstreaming inclusive policy making for inclusive growth 89
Notes 90
References 92

Figures

Figure 1.1. A shift towards inclusive growth 12
Figure 1.2. Income growth for selected social groups 13
Figure 1.3. A shift towards inclusive growth 14
Figure 1.4. Governance implications of inclusive growth policies 17
Figure 1.5. Policy making and policy shaping for inclusive growth 18
Figure 2.1. A strategic policy cycle for Inclusive growth 30
Figure 2.2. The OECD well-being framework 33
Figure 2.3. Regional disparities in life expectancies at birth 36
Figure 2.4. Types of impacts integrated into RIA (December 2014) 42
Figure 3.1. Inclusive Institutions help shape inclusive growth outcomes 64
Figure 3.2. When do consultations happen on primary and subordinate regulations? (2014) 70
Figure 3.3. Levels of stakeholder engagement 73
Figure 3.4. Types of consultation in regulatory policy (December 2014) 74
Figure 3.5. Strengths and weaknesses of engagement mechanisms: Examples from the water sector 76
Figure 3.6. Use of social media in OECD countries 79
Figure 3.7. Obligation of regulators to provide feedback on comments (December 2014) 84
Figure 3.8. Share of central government jobs filled by women, by occupation groups (2010) 88

Tables

Table 2.1. Including inclusive growth considerations in budget impact assessments 39
Table 2.2. Ex post evaluation of inclusive growth policies 54

Executive summary

Slow growth, high unemployment and widening inequalities are at the heart of the policy debate in many parts of the world. Central to this debate is the ability of governments to achieve inclusive growth: that is, to put in place policies that deliver stronger economic growth together with a more even distribution of the benefits of increased prosperity among social groups. These benefits go beyond income to include outcomes across the different dimensions of societal well-being, such as jobs and health.

Public governance, through the principles and mechanisms driving decisions, underpins sound, sustainable policy making for inclusive growth. While many tools and processes are already in place to help policy makers in this endeavour, a more co-ordinated approach is needed to strengthen public governance for inclusive growth. New approaches to policy making are needed that allow governments to better manage complexity, identify policy trade-offs, and promote policy complementarities across sectors (economic, social, environment etc.) and levels of government.

Pursuing inclusive growth outcomes requires a whole-of-government approach that aligns vision, incentives and delivery mechanisms across the policy-making cycle. A strong centre of government, medium-term budgetary considerations and comprehensive tools for assessing the distributional impact of policies are among the key requirements for policy making for inclusive growth. Moreover, inclusive institutions are vital for shaping policies that meet society's needs. Openness and accountability in decision-making ensure that the needs, preferences and concerns of stakeholders, including underserved populations, are taken into account. Efforts to ensure that policies reflect public, rather than special, interests also help achieve inclusive growth objectives.

Many countries are developing frameworks to identify policy objectives that cross traditional sectoral boundaries, but their use in policy making remains limited at both the national and subnational levels. For example, well-being-based frameworks help define policy objectives based on factors that matter for people's life satisfaction, such as income, jobs, health, social capital and participation in public life. But translating these multidimensional objectives into concrete policies and services requires co-ordinated efforts that straddle policy areas, administrative boundaries and levels of government.

The centre of government plays a strong convening and steering role, which is essential in such a multidimensional framework. However, the centre's influence varies significantly across countries, with only a minority exercising high influence over line ministries. There is potential to enhance this leadership and co-ordination role to strengthen concerted government-wide action for inclusive growth.

While many countries have bolstered the evidence base for policy making, more can be done. Some governments already use key national indicators to guide priority setting and policy design. However, more information is needed on the distributional impacts of policies across different social groups and locations, so that a broader set of indicators can be identified for policy design and implementation in the pursuit of inclusive growth.

Several policy instruments are available for aligning inclusive growth objectives with resource allocation over different time horizons. They include medium-term expenditure frameworks and performance-related budgeting, as well as evaluative tools, such as budget and regulatory impact assessments, and expenditure appraisals for both current and capital spending. These instruments are already used widely in many countries, but can be used in a more concerted, systematic way to help identify trade-offs and complementarities and evaluate impacts on a wide variety of social groups. Making the most of these tools, through guidelines, methodological frameworks and capacity building, is particularly important.

New approaches to service delivery, for example using digital technology or partnerships with non-government actors, are especially useful for attaining inclusive growth objectives and can be used more widely. These approaches can help make public services better and more accessible while empowering beneficiaries and communities. However, to fully exploit the potential of these innovative approaches, governments need to to ensure that they work together, and that the public sector has (and develops) the right skills and competencies. Key among these are strategic planning and partnership management, supported by better data on access to services.

Strengthening available evaluation techniques and extending them into broader areas of public social and economic policy are essential to assess and communicate progress in achieving inclusive growth outcomes, and to know and understand what works and what does not. In addition, work remains to be done to promote a holistic approach to evaluation that integrates ex ante and ex post dimensions, and includes inputs from a broad range of institutions, including independent bodies. Multidimensional ex post evaluations have a particular role to play in strengthening accountability for inclusive growth and generating lessons and insights that can inform further policy developments.

Inclusive institutions are essential for shaping inclusive growth policies and outcomes. Countries are increasingly consulting and engaging with the public at different stages of the policy-making cycle. Public engagement, and open government initiatives more broadly, can lead to more effective policies, better-targeted services and stronger accountability. Despite important advances, challenges remain, including under-representation of relevant stakeholders, consultations that occur too late, incomplete processes and weak administrative capacity to carry out participatory processes. More evidence is also needed on the impact of engagement efforts on inclusive policy making.

Averting policy capture – where certain special interests exert undue influence over the policy-making process – is crucial for achieving and sustaining inclusive growth. Governments are making progress in this area, and have much to gain from continuing efforts to secure unbiased and inclusive policy making, for example by increasing transparency and integrity in lobbying and conflict of interest management.

Despite laudable initiatives in many countries, more action is needed to make the public sector more inclusive. An inclusive, more diverse public sector can better represent and address the needs of society, offer greater opportunity, and leading to higher levels of public sector engagement and innovation.

The building blocks for policy making for inclusive growth are present, to various degrees, across OECD countries. The principal challenge is to align these building blocks into an integrated framework that sets a new vision for the public sector and enables the delivery of ambitious, whole-of-government policies for inclusive growth outcomes.

Chapter 1.

Pursuing inclusive growth: The Governance Underpinnings

This chapter explains the role that public governance can play not only in increasing economic growth but also in sharing the benefits among different groups of society, including the neediest. Such Inclusive Growth has a multidimensional nature: it requires that all policy-making tools and processes support and reinforce each other. To achieve Inclusive Growth, governments must address integration, societal needs and inequalities. New approaches are necessary to ensure sustainable policy making; the authors of this chapter present, in particular, an integrated governance approach. They conclude by presenting drivers of reform that align with incentives for the political economy and government priorities.

A shift towards inclusive growth

The OECD defines inclusive growth as "economic growth that creates opportunity for all segments of the population and distributes the dividends of increased prosperity, both in monetary and non-monetary terms, fairly across society".

Growing attention to inclusive growth[1] is motivated to a large extent by rising inequalities in many parts of the world.

Indeed, income inequality has grown rapidly in OECD countries over the last three decades: the income of the top 10% of earners is now around ten times that of the bottom 10% on average in OECD countries, up from seven times three decades ago (Figure 1.1) (OECD, 2015a).[2] The incomes of the poor and the middle class have risen less rapidly than that of the better-off, and income gaps have actually widened since the onset of the global crisis (Figure 1.2).

Figure 1.1. A shift towards inclusive growth

Gini coefficients of income inequality, 1985 and 2013, or latest date available

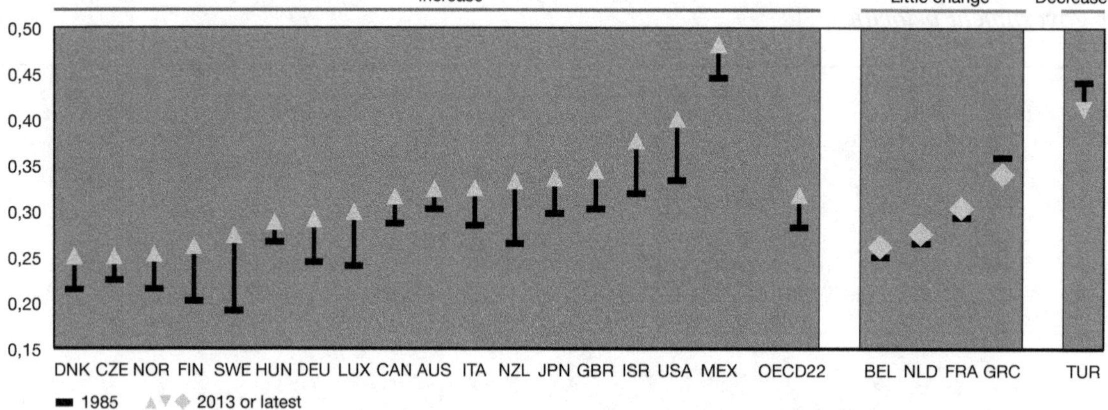

Note: "Little change" in inequality refers to changes of less than 1.5 percentage points. Data for some OECD countries are not available or comparable. Grey squares refer to 2013 or latest dates available. Income is based on the distribution of the equivalised disposable (i.e. after transfers and taxes) household income. Income refers to cash income – excluding imputed components such as home production and imputed rents – regularly received over the year. The analysis refers to the distribution among individuals, while keeping the household as the unit within which income sources are pooled and equally shared. This implies that the income of the household is attributed to each of its members, irrespectively of who in the household receives that income. Data for the Czech Republic and Hungary refer to 1991 instead of 1985.

Source: OECD Income Distribution Database.

Outside the OECD area, in many countries, including China, India and Indonesia, increased prosperity as a result of strong growth in gross domestic product (GDP) has been accompanied by a concentration of income among the well-off, despite drastic reductions in poverty (OECD, 2014a). Moreover, from the mid-1970s to the period immediately preceding the crisis, the top 1% of earners accumulated 47% of total income growth in the United States, 37% in Canada and about 20% in Australia and the United Kingdom (OECD, 2014b).

In addition to rising income inequality, the crisis has also led to a marked increase in poverty in many OECD countries.

Between 2007 and 2011, anchored poverty (calculated by fixing the real low income benchmark at pre-crisis levels) more than doubled in Greece, to 27% of the population, and in Spain, to 18% of the population. There has also been a shift in the age profile of the poor, with rising poverty rates among children and especially youth (OECD, 2015a).

Figure 1.2 Income growth for selected social groups

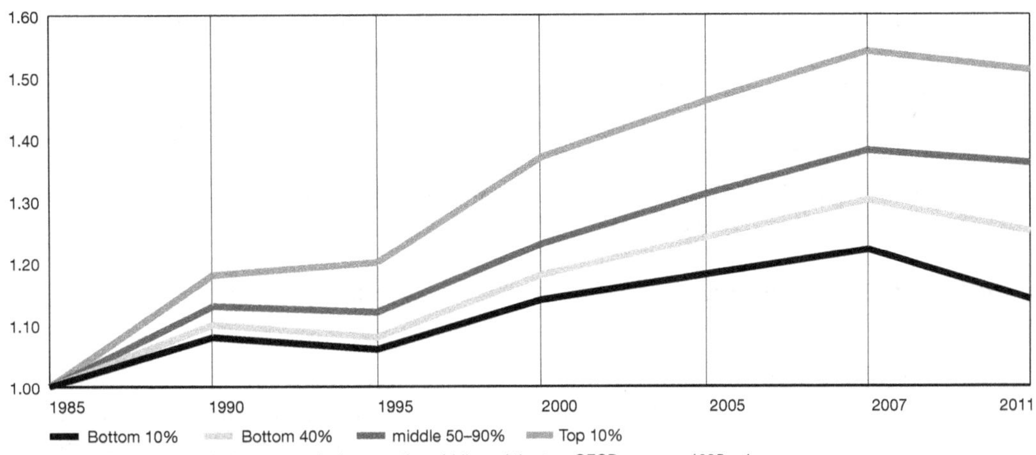

Trends in real household incomes at the bottom, the middle and the top, OECD average, 1985 = 1.

Note: Income refers to disposable household income, corrected for household size. OECD is the unweighted average of 17 countries (Canada, Denmark, Finland, France, Germany, Greece, Israel, Italy, Japan, Luxembourg, Mexico, Netherlands, Norway, New Zealand, Sweden, United Kingdom and United States).

Source: OECD (2015a).

Inclusive growth can be a question of life and death. Better-educated individuals live on average 6 years more than their poorly educated peers.

But inequality is a multidimensional phenomenon that goes far beyond income.

Employment, job satisfaction, health outcomes and educational opportunities matter for people's well-being and are heavily conditioned by socio-economic status or even place-based considerations. In the wake of the crisis, disadvantaged groups, such as the young, have borne the brunt of increased unemployment, non-standard working arrangements have proliferated and around 8% of the working-age population in OECD countries is currently affected by in-work poverty. Within countries[3] a difference in unemployment rate of 32 percentage points can be found between regions in the OECD area, almost twice as high as the difference between the best and worst performing OECD countries. Moreover, the most disadvantaged often live shorter lives and find it difficult to break away from a vicious circle of educational underachievement, low skills and poor employment prospects. By contrast, better educated individuals live longer, on average six years more than their poorly educated peers (OECD, 2013a). Likewise, self-reported health status is higher among the top 20% of income earners than for the bottom 20%,[4] and low-income individuals are more likely to report unmet health care needs (OECD, 2014a).

Inequality is costly and can undermine growth. The increase in income inequality observed in most OECD countries may have thwarted economic growth in those countries.

High levels of inequality can entail large costs.

The relationship between growth and income inequality is complex: growth in material living standards affects income inequality, but the reverse is also true, so that the distribution of the benefits of growth affects future prosperity. Indeed, the increase in income inequality that has taken place in most OECD countries over the last few decades may have thwarted economic growth in those countries (OECD, 2014c)[5] In addition, high levels of inequality can have large social costs, including those due to reduced social cohesion. Just as importantly, rising inequalities can erode confidence in public institutions and in democratic processes and values. Indeed, levels of trust in government have declined in recent years across many OECD countries, posing a challenge for policy in the years to come (OECD, 2013b).

To address these challenges, a shift is needed, as reflected in ongoing OECD work.

Conventionally, policy analysis and advice have focused on improving the population's income and consumption possibilities as a standard gauge of performance, and have measured progress at the level of an "average" individual or household. In other words, emphasising "average economic growth" (such as GDP per capita) as a measure of performance relies on the assumption that the benefits of growth will necessarily trickle down to all social groups and deliver higher welfare to people. Recent research has challenged this assumption, calling for a shift from the traditional binary approach of either growth or redistribution toward "win-win" policies where growth and equity go hand in hand (Figure 1.3). Moreover, this shift is not only conceptual but also has practical implications for every aspect of public policy, as will be outlined in the following chapters. Finally, it is in line with the Sustainable Development Goals that will drive development outcomes for the coming years. These goals include to "promote sustained, inclusive and sustainable economic growth" and to "promote peaceful and inclusive societies for sustainable development".

Figure 1.3. A shift towards inclusive growth

The OECD work on inclusive growth

Working on the trends and policy drivers of inclusive growth.

The OECD approach to inclusive growth has three main aspects: multidimensionality, a focus on distributional considerations and policy impact. In particular:

- What kind of growth? Multidimensionality recognises the importance, when assessing policy impact, of going beyond income to include dimensions that also matter for people's well-being and for their productive participation in the economy and society, such as jobs and health. Indeed, growth in income and material living standards may not lead to improvements in all dimensions of well-being. In other words, increased material prosperity as a result of economic growth may not necessarily translate into better non-income outcomes, such as greater job satisfaction and higher life expectancy.[6]
- Whose growth? Performance is most commonly gauged on the basis of "average" outcomes, or those that are measured for "representative" individuals or households, rather than looking at the full distribution of outcomes across social groups and regions or cities within countries. Instead, inclusive growth stresses the need to assess policy impacts (on income and other dimensions of well-being) not only at the mean, but also along the distribution, including the median household (the "middle class"), the poor and the well-off.
- What outcomes? Conventional analysis looks at the effects of policies on selected outcomes separately. Instead, attention to multidimensionality and distributional considerations requires a broader approach to the evaluation of policy impacts. A better understanding of the causal links between policies and outcomes in various areas can help policy makers identify and exploit synergies among mutually-reinforcing policy levers and to take compensatory action when trade-offs are identified.

How you define growth is essential. When focusing on growth, policy makers must ask themselves: what kind of growth, growth for whom and what are the desired outcomes?

The governance underpinnings of inclusive growth

Public governance plays an essential role in achieving economic growth and narrowing inequality, both directly and indirectly.

Public governance can be thought of as the system of strategic processes and tools, as well as institutions, rules and interactions for effective policy making. Governance failures can lead to widespread informality in the labour market, as well as to limited access to education or to formal safety nets, such as unemployment and health insurance, all of which are drivers of inequalities. Also, government capacity and quality have strong effects on almost all standard measures of well-being, as well as social trust and political legitimacy (Box 1.1). Moreover, through its impact on the quality of public spending and investment and the efficiency of service delivery, public governance can strengthen or undermine the impact of economic policies aimed at inclusive growth.

The notion of well-being is important in measuring the quality of growth. Multidimensional growth criteria include dimensions that matter to people's well-being, e.g. jobs, job quality, educational quality and health.

Box 1.1 Governance matters for achieving inclusive growth

There is a broad consensus, supported by evidence, that good governance is vital for a number of key outcomes at the national and subnational levels, including social cohesion, public expenditure efficiency and control of corruption. In addition, governance matters for achieving sustainable, inclusive economic growth. Coase (1960) argues that good institutions, such as strong property rights, reduce transaction costs and consequently support economic development. Similarly, North (1991) contends that institutions that strengthen contract enforcement are necessary to economic development. More recently, Rodrik, Subramanian and Trebbi (2004) find that the quality of institutions is more important for growth than geography or trade. Other scholars (e.g. Acemoglu and Robinson, 2008) argue that institutions, including an efficient public sector and absence of corruption, are fundamental drivers of economic growth.

Governance also matters for inclusiveness. Inclusive institutions ensure that markets are functional and open to competition, and allow for broad citizen participation, pluralism and an effective system of checks and balances, leading to better access to services and opportunity. In that respect, cross-country evidence shows that inclusive governance can improve development outcomes, such as better literacy and health, or lower infant mortality (e.g. Halperin, Siegle and Weinstein, 2010: Evans and Ferguson, 2013). Rajkumar and Swaroop (2002) also find that, for example, corruption disproportionately denies the poor access to education and health services.

Public governance is an essential lever for high-impact public spending, which in turn enhances the potential of economic policies aimed at inclusive growth. For example, stakeholder engagement and consultation can help identify needs and preferences, better targeting government programmes and increasing efficiency. Public governance also affects the quality and efficiency of public investment. In this respect, strengthening inclusive institutions has a great potential to enhance citizen participation, provide better public services, reduce transaction costs, and – ultimately – reduce inequalities while promoting economic growth.

Last, but not least, governance matters for well-being. People are more satisfied with their lives in countries with better-quality governance. More importantly, changes in the way policies are designed and delivered affect quality of life. Changes in average life evaluations in 157 countries over 2005-12 can be explained as much by changes in governance quality as by changes in GDP, even though some of the benefits of better governance come from increases in economic efficiency. The well-being payoff of improved governance in that period can be compared to a 40% increase in per capita incomes (OECD, 2014d).

Fragmented systems of public governance hinder inclusiveness, facilitating avoidable trade-offs and co-ordination failures.

Public governance is important throughout the policy-making cycle, in the design, implementation and evaluation of inclusive growth policies.

A defining feature of inclusive growth is multidimensionality, meaning that both income and non-income considerations are taken into account in defining intended outcomes. This requires that governments have the capacity to deal with complexity in policy making, assess policy impacts from broader viewpoints, and identify complementarities and trade-offs among and within policies and policy objectives.

avoidable trade-offs and co-ordination failures within and across administrative boundaries. In order to ensure that policies are aligned, governments need a range of tools and processes that improve co-ordination across sectors and levels of government. Last but not least, achieving inclusive growth starts with the right definition of needs and expectations, anchored in an inclusive policy-making process (Figure 1.4).

Figure 1.4 Governance implications of inclusive growth policies

Inclusive Growth policies	Governance implications
Focus on multidimensional policy impacts: material living and non-material living standards	• Shaping a vision for Inclusive Growth: guiding the definition of Inclusive Growth goals with reliable, timely multidimensional data • Enhanced policy coherence: assess and address trade-offs and complementarities between multidimensional policy objectives
Focus on integrated policies: growth and redistribution	• Sustained implementation efforts: anticipating broader socio economic changes that may inform Inclusive Growth (IG) targets, and aligning short, medium and longer-term resource and priority considerations • Assessing multidimensional impact: using ex ante evaluation to assess distributional impact along with economic impact • Assessing impact and strengthening feedback: reinforcing accountability and evaluation mechanisms to capture Inclusive Growth targets
Focus on outcomes that reflect the needs of societies (health, education, jobs)	• Whole-of-government approach: targeting joined-up outcomes beyond administrative silos, encouraging policies to reinforce each other, and a strong co-ordinating role for the centre of government • Quality decision making: promoting balanced participation through stakeholder engagement and mechanisms to prevent capture in decision-making, and encouraging inclusive problem identification • Multilevel governance: aligning outcomes at higher and lower levels of government to improve coherence of public policy
Focus on inequalities (income and well-being) and on different social groups and scales beyond the average	• Inclusive service delivery: implementation that seeks to maximise access, use and responsiveness across social groups and locations • Inclusive engagement: feedback and engagement mechanisms to promote an inclusive policy implementation process • Access to redress: providing the possibility of enforcing a right or redressing a wrong to enable opportunity • Multilevel analysis: including place-based considerations that may drive inequalities

Source: OECD.

Policy making for inclusive growth: an integrated governance approach

Pursuing inclusive growth calls for a whole-of-government approach that leverages informed decision-making and aligns vision, incentives and delivery mechanisms across the policy-making cycle.

The public governance underpinnings of inclusive growth can be tackled from a double perspective: policy making, where public sector strategies, tools and processes are strengthened and aligned towards inclusive growth outcomes across the policy-making cycle, and policy-shaping, where openness, accountability and inclusion are brought to bear in problem definition, delivery and implementation (Figure 1.5).

Inclusive growth outcomes require coherent action across the policy cycle, from design and implementation to evaluation.

Figure 1.5 Policy making and policy shaping for inclusive growth

Policy Design
- Inclusive Growth challenges are understood and forecasted
- A whole-of-government vision for Inclusive Growth steers, aligns the public sector
- Policy frameworks tackle multidimensionality and seek policy coherence across sectors and levels of government
- Solid evidence (ex ante, ex post) assesses distributional impacts

Policy Implementation
- Spending decisions are aligned with medium and longer term Inclusive Growth considerations
- Coordination, whole-of-government steering and accountability mechanisms and enable pursuit of joined-up outcomes
- Innovation in service delivery facilitates access across social groups and locations

Policy Evaluation
- Assessment of distributional impact of outcomes that matter for well-being
- Responsive changes are made based on beneficiary assessment of services & service providers
- Comprehensive evaluation approaches and feedback loops inform new policy packages, including from independent audit and control mechanisms

Inclusive Institutions for Inclusive Policy Making
- Openness and engagement support inclusive problem identification and decision making
- Transparency and integrity tools help avert policy decisions that benefit the few
- Participatory mechanisms promote an inclusive policy implementation process
- Inclusive public sector workforce reflects society and can better engage in delivering
- Access to dispute resolution enables opportunities, particularly of vulnerable groups

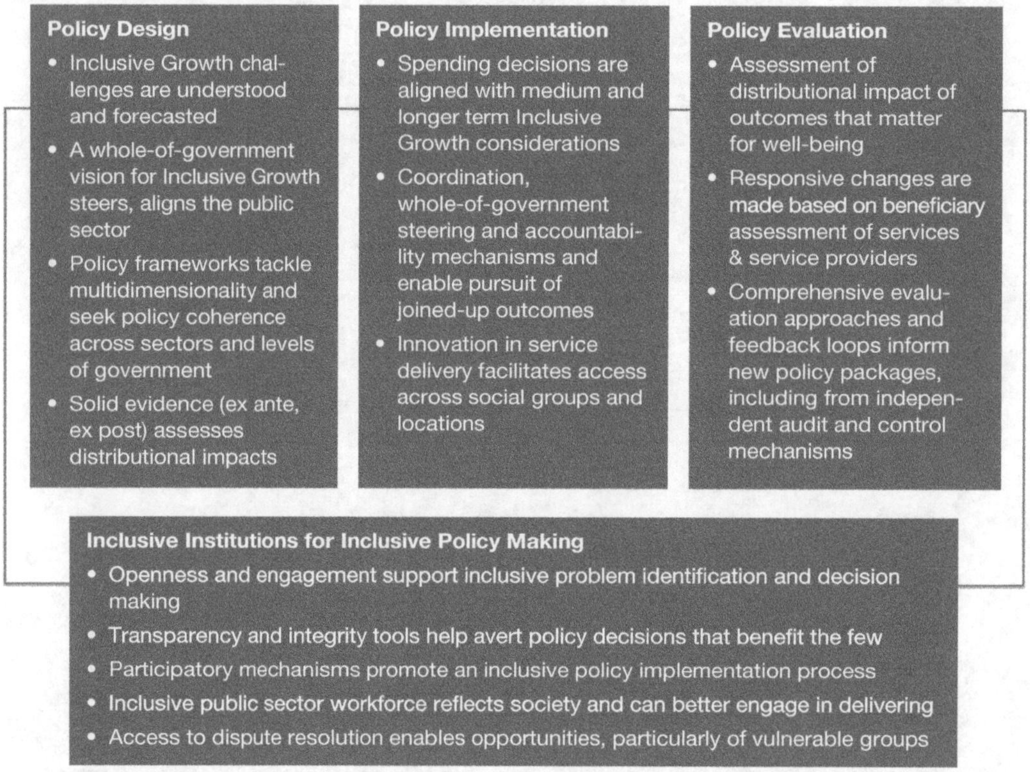

Once the vision for inclusive growth is defined, specific institutions and tools can be leveraged to design, implement and evaluate inclusive growth policies.

Aligning objectives and facilitating their delivery through improved coherence and co-ordination across policy areas and levels of government must be part of this process. This includes, for example:

- Better understanding and forecasting demand.

- Facilitating the assessment of policy trade-offs and complementarities through evidence-based decision-making (e.g. ex ante regulatory impact assessment and ex post evaluation).
- Enabling the required co-ordination and alignment across sectors and administrative organisations (e.g. centre of government) to deliver joined-up outcomes.
- Anchoring implementation with built-in incentives (e.g. budget)
- Capacities to support implementation of inclusive growth policies (e.g. civil service skills, information sharing systems).

These tools and institutions need to be anchored in an enabling political and institutional environment that can shape intended outcomes.

Policies to promote inclusive growth with the needed depth and consistency come from strong, inclusive institutions. By embracing openness and accountability in decision-making, governments can ensure that the needs and concerns of underserved populations are reflected in policy decisions, particularly in relation to powerful, well-organised interest groups. In addition, meaningful stakeholder engagement can lead to better targeted, more effective policies and policy implementation. A policy-making process that is informed, inclusive and designed to aggregate competing interests can help ensure that citizens' well-being is a central factor in economic policy making.

> ***By embracing openness and accountability, governments can ensure that the needs of underserved populations are reflected in policy decisions.***

Public governance mechanisms and processes can enhance the capacity of policy makers to design, implement and evaluate inclusive growth policy packages, as well as the underlying institutional delivery frameworks.

Embedding both the right tools and processes, together with the principles of openness and inclusion across the policy cycle, from policy design to implementation and evaluation, can provide an essential foundation for more inclusive institutions that deliver more inclusive policy outcomes (Annex I). In particular:

- Renewed attention to policy design can help address the complexities of targeting multidimensional outcomes and assessing trade-offs and complementarities. A whole-of-government approach to inclusive growth begins with a strong, compelling vision of what the challenges and opportunities are, and what the desired outcomes should be. For this, policy makers require a good understanding of needs and expectations across different societal groups and place-based considerations and access to timely, evidence-based information to objectively frame inclusive growth challenges and prioritise policy actions. Governments can use a variety of instruments to strengthen the evidence base for inclusive growth policy making, including regulatory impact assessments (RIA), forecasting or cost-benefit analysis, and short- and longer-term goals, including sectorial and/or regional strategies and medium- term expenditure frameworks. These tools clarify the effects and the trade-offs of government actions for decision-makers and stakeholders alike and, when used systematically, provide strong levers for governments to identify and target social inclusiveness goals.

- Aligning vision with resources and capacities through effective policy implementation is essential for delivering joined-up outcomes. Mainstreaming an inclusive growth perspective that cuts across administrative silos and levels of government can be supported by ad hoc monitoring and accountability mechanisms (e.g. sector-wide accountability frameworks), measures to promote and reward progress, as well as horizontal co-ordination and co-operation. In addition, in a context where governments must maximise the impact, reach and quality of public services, new approaches to service delivery hold a number of opportunities. New forms of partnership and alternative service provision mechanisms, as long as they are anchored in transparency and accountability, can help deliver better results for citizens at a reduced cost for government, while digital innovation can improve accessibility and evidence-based decision making.
- A focus on multidimensional policy evaluation is essential for assessing and communicating progress in delivering inclusive growth outcomes. In a context of high expectations but limited resources, evaluation is an important part of refining public policies, particularly in areas of heavy public spending and those closely associated with inclusiveness. Together with performance information, a solid ex post evaluation system focused on social outcomes can provide invaluable feedback to inform budget decisions and overall policy priorities. Underlying these tools is the need for reliable, timely data, including on beneficiaries and intermediaries, and for independent institutions (e.g. productivity commissions, national evaluation agencies or supreme audit institutions).

Inclusive institutions can boost the impact of these tools and processes as enablers of inclusive growth policy making.

Stakeholder engagement can increases the likelihood of policy outcomes that deliver for the many, not just the few. Similarly, actively engaging stakeholders in monitoring service delivery, regulatory outcomes and budget execution can help guide and ensure effective implementation. There is increasing evidence that collaboration with citizens and service users can help tackle service failure and drive innovation. Likewise, accountability and evaluation can be strengthened through engagement and participatory mechanisms. For example, participatory evaluation places stakeholders at the centre of assessing the success of policies and programmes; it can improve the usefulness of evaluation results, as it increases the likelihood that the outcomes of an evaluation will be relevant for stakeholders and used as a basis for future actions. In addition, an inclusive public sector workforce can leverage talent, promote innovation and improve service delivery, particularly at the front-line. The implications of inclusiveness for processes, institutions, and issues of culture and capacity within public administration and policy making are important elements of public governance for inclusive growth.

Stakeholder engagement increases the likelihood of policy outcomes that deliver for the many, not just the few.

Parliaments can also provide valuable input into the policy-making process.

As elected representatives of the people, parliaments can add legitimacy and authenticity in raising the concerns of citizens and marginalised social groups in ways that transcend the role of other bodies. The role of parliaments in policy making for inclusive growth can be further enhanced with good information flows and dialogue between elected representatives and civil society.

Finally, improving access to justice is increasingly recognised as an important means to tackle inequality and contribute to inclusive growth.[7]

The inability to access justice services can be both a result and a cause of disadvantage. Further, legal problems tend to occur in combination, creating clusters of legal needs (housing, employment) and compounding legal issues. Lack of their resolution can, in turn, reinforce social exclusion and inequalities for those who have neither the means nor the ability to effectively solve their legal problems. In addition, the inability to resolve legal problems can deny access to economic opportunity and undermine human potential.[8,9] Indeed, there is increasing evidence that unresolved legal problems and inadequate access to justice can be costly for both the individual and society at large. Costs of inaccessible justice may stem from stress and health effects, loss of income and loss of employment.[10] While principally an issue for lower-income groups, there is also concern that an adequate access to justice increasingly affects middle income households.[11] Providing suitable access to legal and justice services can play a crucial role in helping people move out of social exclusion and enable equal access to economic opportunities.

The political economy of inclusive growth: Reform does not happen passively, it depends on the legitimacy, leadership and impetus of government for its success.

OECD analysis on the drivers of successful reform (OECD, 2010) provides grounds for optimism that the agenda of inclusive growth – as elaborated in subsequent chapters – aligns well with the political economy incentives and priorities of government. In particular:

The 6 habits of highly successful reforms

OECD analysis has established a list of criteria for successful reform that are directly applicable to Inclusive growth objectives.

Pursuing inclusive growth: The governance underpinnings

1. A clear popular mandate for reform. The dimensions of Inclusive growth – the various aspects of well-being, notably quality of education, health care and the environment, as well as household income – correspond directly with the substance of economic and social discourse. In other words, Inclusive growth is concerned with what really matters to people, and in turn to their public representatives.
2. An evidence-based and analytically sound case for reform. Persuading and convincing citizens – and indeed politicians and the policy-making community more generally – of the case for Inclusive growth reform is greatly facilitated through access to evidence and analysis that demonstrates the benefits (Chapter 2).
3. Strong leadership. Inclusive growth objectives – which by their nature have a multidimensional nature and a whole-of-government character – are naturally

within the leadership domain of the centre of government, which is best placed both to articulate and to oversee delivery of these goals (Chapter 2).

4. Clear communication of reform objectives and inclusive, consultative processes. The articulation of medium-term well-being objectives, via Key National Indicators and National Performance Frameworks, allows for open and consultative engagement with societal stakeholders to build a vision of Inclusive growth (Chapter 3).
5. Demonstrate continual progress over time. Inclusive growth is a substantive, medium- and longer-term policy objective that has the potential to transform citizen's experiences for the better. Tracking these medium-term objectives over time, within a responsive multi-annual policy cycle, underpins the government's seriousness-of-purpose in pursuing an Inclusive growth agenda.
6. Keeping stakeholders on board over time. In a similar vein, multi-annual outcome tracking allows for the views, insights and critiques of stakeholders to be continually sought and assessed throughout the policy cycle, with feedback and accountability regarding the impacts of the Inclusive growth programme (Chapter 3).

Country experience is instructive.

For example, Finland's experience in carrying forward various reform agendas – now proposed to be streamlined within a "Blueprint for Reform" (OECD, 2015b) – illustrates how these various elements can be brought together to forge a consensus on national reform and its delivery. Notable features of Finland's case include strong leadership from the centre of government (overcoming the potential challenges of a multiparty coalition), a strong focus on "strategic implementation" (with various sectors, projects and measures grouped under three overarching policy objectives) and close attention to evidence- based analysis.

Ultimately, inclusive growth will only gain traction if it commands the attention of the public and of policy makers as an appropriate frame of reference for designing policies for the betterment of society.

The following chapters will elaborate on why, and how inclusive growth can serve such a role.

Notes

1 The OECD considers inclusive growth as "economic growth that creates opportunity for all segments of the population and distributes the dividends of increased prosperity, both in monetary and non-monetary terms, fairly across society" (OECD, 2014a).

2 OECD Income Distribution Database: www.oecd.org/els/soc/income-distribution-database.htm.

3 OECD Regional Wellbeing Database: www.oecdregionalwellbeing.org/.

4 OECD Statistical Database: http://stats.oecd.org.

5 For example, between 1990 and 2010, rising inequality is estimated to have knocked more than ten percentage points off growth in Mexico, nearly nine points in Finland, Norway and the United Kingdom, and between six and seven points in Italy, Sweden and the United States (OECD, 2014e).

6 Indeed, the cross-country correlation between growth rates of GDP per capita and multidimensional living standards is positive but with large variance across countries. For example, France and Germany have registered almost the same per capita GDP growth during 1995-2007, but living standards grew 1.7 times faster in France. Of this variance in multidimensional living standards, only 38% can be statistically explained by GDP growth. One element that shapes these differences is the divergence between GDP growth and the growth of average household income, influenced by structural factors such as the fiscal stance or the respective roles of the private and public sectors (OECD, 2014a).

7 OECD (2014a); see also US Department of Justice (2014), "Interagency Legal Aid Roundtable Toolkit" www.justice.gov/atj/legal-aid-interagency-roundtable-toolkit; remarks of Director Lisa Foster, US Access to Justice Initiative, Equal Justice Conference May 2015; Gargarella, R. "Too far removed from the people", Access to Justice for the Poor: The Case of Latin America; Canadian Forum on Civil Justice (2006) Social, Economic and Health Problems Associated with a Lack of Access to the Courts, A special report from the Civil Justice System and the Public Project, Commissioned by the Research and Statistics Division, Department of Justice Canada. March; Currie A., The Legal Problems of Everyday Life, The Nature, Extent and Consequences of Justiciable Problems Experienced by Canadians, Department of Justice Canada; Indiana Legal Services, Inc., the Indiana Bar Foundation, and the Pro Bono Committee of the Indiana State Bar Association (Indiana Legal Services & al.) (2008), Unequal Access to Justice: A Comprehensive Study of the Civil Legal Needs of the Poor in Indiana.

8 Beqiraj J., McNamara L. (2014), International Access to Justice: Barriers and Solutions (Bingham Centre for the Rule of Law Report 02/2014), International Bar Association; Sharon Matthews, Making the case for the economic value of legal aid, Briefing note (Canadian Bar Association, British Colombian branch); Canadian Forum on Civil Justice (2006) Social, Economic and Health Problems Associated with a Lack of Access to the Courts, A special report from the Civil Justice System and the Public Project, Commissioned by the Research and Statistics Division, Department of Justice Canada.

9 OECD (2006), "Chapter 5. Enhancing Women's Market Access and Promoting Pro-Poor Growth", Promoting Pro-Poor Growth: Guidance for Donors, DAC Guidelines and Reference Series, OECD Publishing, Paris.

10 Some estimates show that, for example in the United Kingdom, each legal problem reported to cause physical illness may ultimately cost the healthcare system between 113-528 GBP and between 195-2 224 GBP per patient in stress-related effects. Estimates from England and Wales indicate that unresolved legal problems cost individuals and the public 13 billion GBP over a 3.5 year period. On the impact of legal aid, studies point out that it can save public funds by reducing evictions and alleviating homelessness, protecting patient health and helping low-income people participate in federal safety-net programmes. Legal aid can also contribute to

economic growth by increasing jobs, reducing work days missed due to legal problems, creating more stable housing, resolving debt issues and stimulating business activity. For example, a 2009 Texas study found that for every direct dollar in legal aid, the annual gains to the economy were found to be reduction of 7.42 USD in total spending and gains of 3.52 USD in output, and 2.20 USD in personal income. See amongst others, Pleasence, Buck and Balmer, 2006; Stratton and Anderson, 2008; Abel, 2012; The Perryman Group, 2009.

11 There is no agreed on methodological approach for measuring citizen legal needs and costs of accessing justice.

References

Abel, L. K. (2012), Economic Benefits of Civil Legal Aid, National Centre for Access to Justice, Cardoza Law School, 4 September, https://ncforaj.files.wordpress.com/2012/09/final-economic-benefits-of-legal-aid-9-5-2012.pdf

Acemoglu, D. and J. Robinson (2008), The Role of Institutions in Growth and Development, The International Bank for Reconstruction and Development/The World Bank.

Beqiraj, J. and L. McNamara (2014), "International access to justice: Barriers and solutions", Bingham Centre for the Rule of Law Report 02/2014, International Bar Association.

Canadian Forum on Civil Justice (2006), Social, Economic and Health Problems Associated with a Lack of Access to the Courts, a special report from the Civil Justice System and the Public Project, commissioned by the Research and Statistics Division, Department of Justice Canada, March.

Coase, R. H. (1960), "The problem of social cost", Journal of Law and Economics, pp. 1-44.

Evans, W. and C. Ferguson (2013), Governance, Institutions, Growth and Poverty Reduction: A Literature Review, Department for International Development, London.

Halperin, M., J. Siegle and M. Weinstein (2010), The Democracy Advantage: How Democracies Promote Prosperity and Peace, revised edition, Routledge, Abingdon.

Indiana Legal Services, Inc., Indiana Bar Foundation and Pro Bono Committee of the Indiana State Bar Association (2008), Unequal Access to Justice: A Comprehensive Study of the Civil Legal Needs of the Poor in Indiana.

OECD (2015a), *In It Together: Why Less Inequality Benefits All*, OECD Publishing, Paris, http://dx.doi.org/10.1787/9789264235120-en.

OECD (2015b), *Slovak Republic: Better Co-ordination for Better Policies, Services and Results*, OECD Public Governance Reviews, OECD Publishing, Paris, http://dx.doi.org/10.1787/9789264247635-en.

OECD (2014a), *All on Board: Making Inclusive Growth Happen*, OECD Publishing, Paris, http://dx.doi.org/10.1787/9789264218512-en.

OECD (2014b), "Focus on top incomes and taxation in OECD countries: Was the crisis a game changer?", OECD Publishing, Paris, www.oecd.org/els/soc/

OECD (2014c), OECD Technical Notes: *Focus on Top Incomes and Taxation in OECD Countries: Was the crisis a game changer?* http://www.oecd.org/els/soc/OECD2014-FocusOnTopIncomes.pdf. *Does Income Inequality Hurt Economic Growth?* www.oecd.org/els/soc/Focus-Inequality-and-Growth-2014.pdf

OECD (2014d), *Open government in Latin America*, OECD Public Governance Reviews, OECD Publishing, Paris, http://dx.doi.org/10.1787/9789264223639-en.

OECD (2014e), *OECD Regional Outlook 2014: Regions and Cities: Where Policies and People Meet*, OECD Publishing, Paris, http://dx.doi.org/10.1787/9789264201415-en.

OECD (2013a), *Health at a Glance 2013: OECD Indicators*, OECD Publishing, Paris, http://dx.doi.org/10.1787/health_glance-2013-en.

OECD (2013b), Investing in Trust: Leveraging Institutions for Inclusive Policymaking, OECD, Paris, http://www.oecd.org/gov/ethics/Investing-in-trust.pdf.

OECD (2007), "Enhancing Women's Market Access and Promoting Pro-poor Growth", in OECD. , *Promoting Pro-Poor Growth: Policy Guidance for Donors*, OECD Publishing, Paris, http://dx.doi.org/10.1787/9789264024786-12-en

Pleasence, P., A. Buck and N. J. Balmer (eds.) (2006), Transforming Lives: Law and Social Process, Belfast.

Rajkumar and V. Swaroop (2002), "Public spending and outcomes: Does governance matter?", Policy Research Working Paper 2840, World Bank, Washington, DC.

Rodrik, D., A. Subramanian and F. Trebbi (2004), "Institutions rule: The primacy of institutions over geography and integration in economic development", Journal of Economic Growth, 9(2), pp. 131-165.

Stratton and Anderson (2006), Social, Economic and Health Problems Associated with a Lack of Access to the Courts: A special report from the Civil Justice System and the Public Project, Commissioned by the Research and Statistics Division, Department of Justice Canada, http://www.cfcj-fcjc.org/sites/default/files/docs/2008/cjsp-socialproblems-en.pdf

The Perryman Group (2009), The Impact of Legal Aid Services on Economic Activity in Texas: An Analysis of Current Efforts and Expansion Potential, Perryman Group, Waco, February.

US Department of Justice (2014), Legal Aid Interagency Roundtable "Toolkit", www.justice.gov/atj/legal-aid-interagency-roundtable-toolkit.

Chapter 2.

Policy making for inclusive growth: aligning design, delivery and accountability

This chapter examines the tools and processes that serve a strategic policy cycle for Inclusive Growth, applying a whole-of-government approach. Centres of government must co-ordinate complex policies and national priorities and build a shared vision across all levels of government, relying on national and regional indicators. Budgetary governance for Inclusive Growth involves managing trade-offs and aligning resources for strategic multi-year budgeting. Assessment tools, beginning with ex ante evaluations of government expenditure and regulations, can help in shaping policies. The authors explain the benefits for governments of using data visualisation tools and resources in the policy development cycle. They promote government accountability through incentives and horizontal co-ordination. The chapter also presents ways to make service delivery more inclusive, looking at access and reach, digital welfare, and capacity. Finally, it describes how to close the policy cycle with a focus on ex post evaluation, accountability and learning.

Towards a strategic policy cycle

Policy making – the process by which governments make decisions to solve problems and improve socio-economic conditions – is not a single, uniform activity of government.

First, policies go through several stages along the policy cycle, from design to implementation and evaluation. Anchored in a strategic vision for Inclusive growth, a number of tools and processes inform and enable these policy-making stages, including budget, performance and accountability mechanisms. They must work in unison for policies to achieve their intended objectives.

Second, rarely is a policy implemented singlehandedly: responsibility for outcomes is often shared across levels of government, executive agencies or programmes. Last but not least, policies can be delivered through a diverse range of policy tools that governments have at their disposal, from public expenditure, taxation and regulation to joint action (Box 2.1). These may entail trade-offs but also offer opportunities for complementarity.

With multidimensional criteria comes increased complexity. Finding ways for policy-making tools and processes to work together is essential to overcoming complexity and enabling and inclusive growth strategy.

The complexities inherent in policy making are exacerbated in the context of designing, implementing and assessing Inclusive growth policies.

As discussed in Chapter 1, addressing multidimensionality calls for concerted action, whereby all of the policy-making tools and processes work together – throughout the various phases and aspects of the strategic policy cycle – to support and reinforce one another in achieving ambitious, challenging objectives (Figure 2.1).

This chapter accordingly discusses the strong convening, steering and accountability role of the centre of government; the strategic alignment of key policy making tools with broader outcomes, including through medium-term expenditure frameworks (MTEFs) and performance mechanisms; the role of ex ante and ex post evaluation in assessing and informing Inclusive growth policies; as well as maximising impact and reach through innovation in service delivery.

Box 2.1. Policy levers and inclusive growth

Public expenditure entails allocating resources directly to achieve policy objectives via the annual and multi-annual budget processes. Achieving Inclusive growth requires investment in physical infrastructure and human capital, including education, justice and health care. For example, the availability of electricity, water and transport infrastructure, as well as schools and hospitals, has a key impact on inclusiveness. Similarly, the overall pattern and impacts of current expenditures programmes – including, but not limited to, social programmes and support for vulnerable social groups – can profoundly affect Inclusive growth outcomes.

Taxation entails raising revenues to fund government activities and to influence behaviour. Taxation affects the distribution of income among individuals and households through its interaction with benefit systems and can provide incentives and support for particular sectors of the economy. Taxation can also affect outcomes other than income. For example, environmental taxes can raise revenue while also helping to curb pollution, which in turns affects social groups differently.

Regulation entails structuring and changing the legal environment, including administrative procedures and requirements, to control and influence markets, as well as business and citizen behaviour. Together with public expenditure and taxation, regulation is a key lever in ensuring welfare and economic prosperity. A tool, such as the regulatory impact assessment, can help integrate the issues of Inclusive growth into the law-making process, revealing policy trade-offs between economic, social and environmental effects of potential regulatory responses.

Joint action entails working with civil society, social partners and other actors to advance commonly-held public policy goals. Achieving Inclusive growth also depends on whether policies integrate perspectives of various stakeholders. Joint action can bring attention to important socio-economic issues, including topics such as human development, equality, pensions and public service delivery. These issues matter for the well-being of citizens and can be particularly effective at empowering vulnerable groups and thus foster Inclusive growth.

Figure 2.1 A strategic policy cycle for inclusive growth

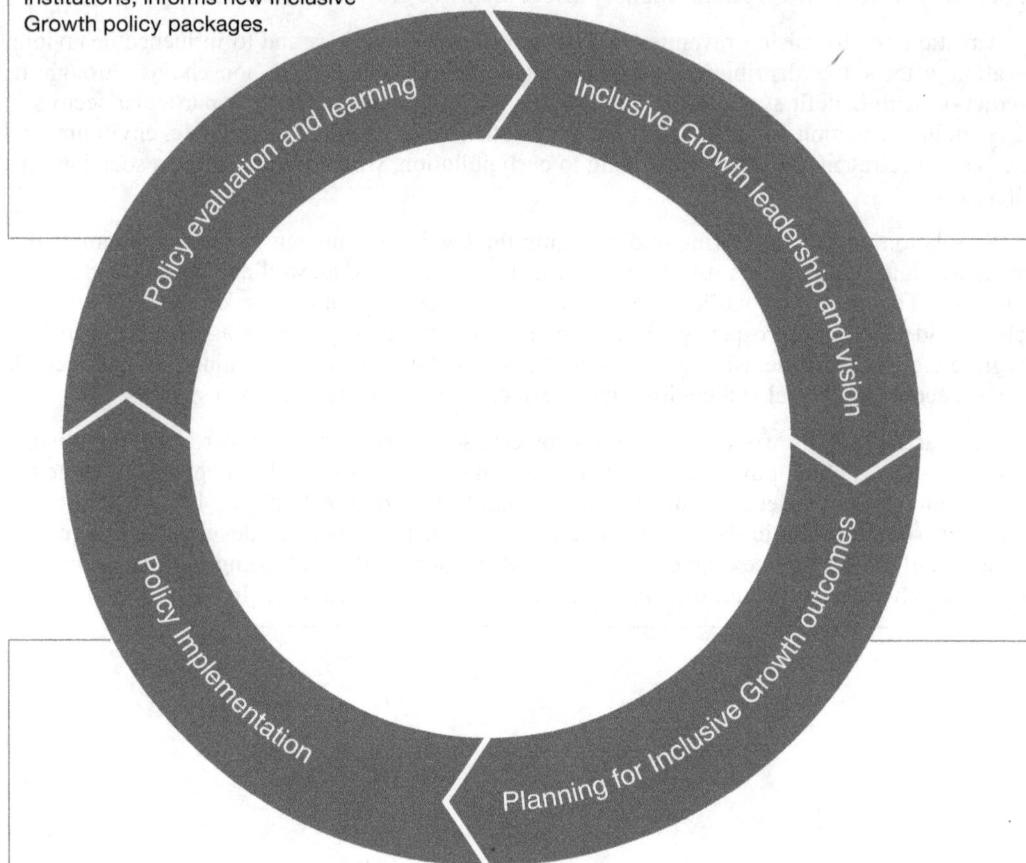

The case for a whole-of-government approach: Fostering co-ordination and the role of centres of government

Policy making for inclusive growth poses new challenges for public governance.

How do government decisions translate into improved services, changed outcomes and better lives for citizens? How do whole-of-government priorities become organisational goals and motivating targets for teams and individuals across policy areas and administrative units? The conventional answer to these questions is that policy making follows a "cascade", whereby the government sets strategic goals that are mapped onto high-level objectives and "output" goals for line ministries and agencies. In turn, these strategic goals are translated into performance targets and specific activity objectives for divisions and individuals. How well these specific goals are met largely determines how well the top-level outcome priorities are achieved. This long-established conception of how policy making works has the merit of simplicity, although there are additional dimensions of complexity that need to be factored in.

> ***How do whole-of-government priorities become organisational goals and motivating targets for teams and individuals across policy areas and administrative units? Inclusive growth often requires a horizontal approach that goes beyond conventional administrative boundaries.***

Steering inclusive growth requires managing a complex policy landscape.

The essential connection between a steering vision and its implementation through activities, outputs and outcomes depends crucially on the "logic model" – the policy rationale for how specific actions feed into achieving the higher- level objectives. How to develop such a logic model is addressed later in this chapter. Second, and just as importantly, the simple "cascade" does not take account of the fact that many higher-level outcomes depend for their success not on a single line of outputs and activities, but on multiple strands and streams of different factors, some of which may be under the control of different bodies. Instead of a cascade, then, the public policy complex may sometimes resemble a system of tributaries and deltas, hard to map and to visualise, and with multiple interconnections.

The centre of government can play a vital role in defining and steering the implementation of a national vision for inclusive growth.

The centre of government (CoG) – Prime Minister's Office, President's Office or Cabinet Office as the case may be – typically acts as the principal co-ordinator of complex policies and national priorities. Among the responsibilities of the CoG is the task to mobilise actors inside and outside government and involve them in setting this vision around key outcomes, as well as in its implementation. Also, the CoG combines, in principle, strategic vision, policy co-ordination authority and monitoring functions and capacity. Because of its placement, by definition outside of line ministries, it can serve as a neutral broker that steers common objectives, rather than specific sectoral agendas while using its proximity to the highest levels of decision-making to convene departments and align policies. Finally, the many tools that the CoG can leverage – and potentially more effectively than at the line ministry level – include holding funding pools and designing accountability frameworks for cross departmental co-operation; supporting departments with centrally located policy units; and conveying key messages and evidence to Cabinet and Head of Government in order to ensure high-level support.

Building a shared vision

Delivering outcomes starts with setting a vision that charts the way and helps align the public sector, but also government and society at large, around shared goals.

A compelling, overarching vision statement enables government to communicate in simple terms, internally and externally, its overarching objectives and the relevance of single- and multi-sector priority initiatives designed to achieve them. This vision needs of course to be aligned with a political mandate, grounded in the democratic process which tests, shapes and determines the priorities of the people. Further, this vision can lead to identifying a set of key national indicators (KNIs), which should infuse and motivate all government action and provide a road map for joined-up delivery.

Increasingly, OECD governments are articulating their ambitions and goals for national well-being.

In a number of countries, governments are aiming to align their vision with a national discussion on the outcomes that matter for people's life satisfaction. Indeed, the OECD has undertaken extensive work on measuring well-being and in designing high-quality indicators that allow the various dimensions of public performance and life-quality to be mapped and measured. These indicators comprise a comprehensive, internationally-comparable suite of outcome measures, which government can draw on as a resource in selecting its priorities, and can be used to benchmark progress in achieving these objectives over time (Figure 2.2) (OECD, 2013a)

Figure 2.2 The OECD well-being framework

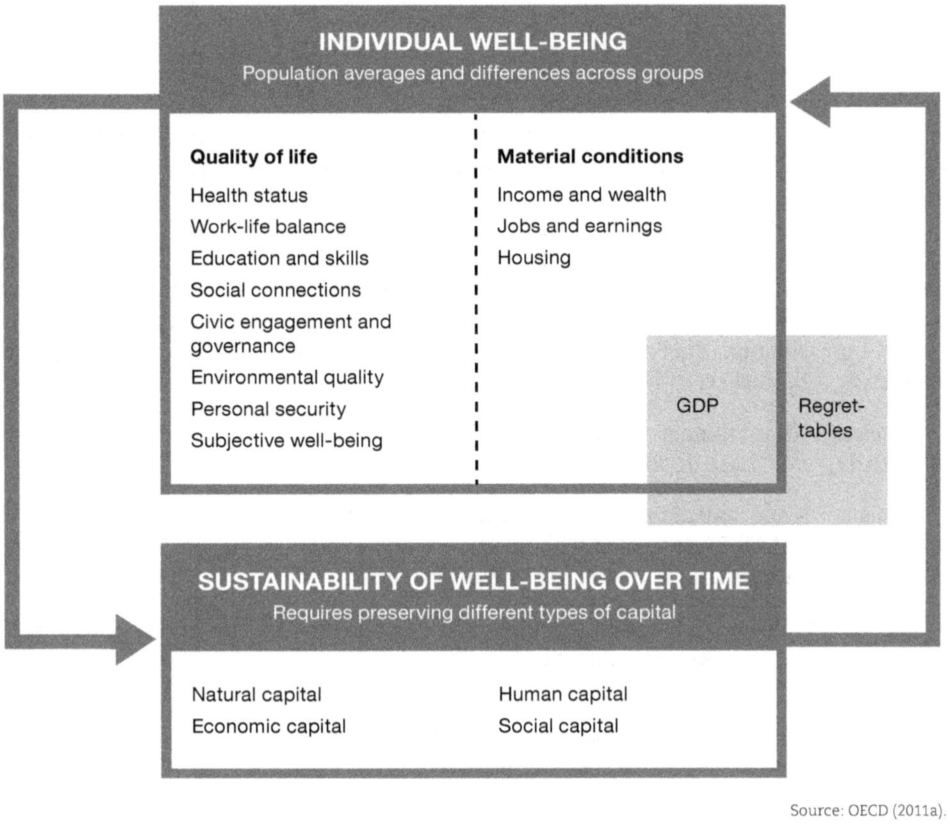

INDIVIDUAL WELL-BEING
Population averages and differences across groups

Quality of life
Health status
Work-life balance
Education and skills
Social connections
Civic engagement and governance
Environmental quality
Personal security
Subjective well-being

Material conditions
Income and wealth
Jobs and earnings
Housing

GDP
Regret-tables

SUSTAINABILITY OF WELL-BEING OVER TIME
Requires preserving different types of capital

Natural capital
Economic capital
Human capital
Social capital

Source: OECD (2011a).

Source: OECD (2011a).

National experiences are particularly instructive in this regard.

For example, France and New Zealand are developing high-level indicators to broaden policy analysis beyond traditional economic metrics and incorporate a well-being perspective in policy making more explicitly. In both countries, the high-level indicators are evolving towards a three-pronged clustering around the themes of (i) economy/prosperity, (ii) social progress/inclusiveness and (iii) sustainability (Box 2.2).

Box 2.2. Key national indicators in budgeting: France and New Zealand

France's performance beyond gross domestic product (GDP) and use of KNIs: France's over-arching budget law (Loi organique relative aux lois des finances or LOLF) provides for grouping public expenditure by "missions", which bring together related policy programmes and which in turn are associated with performance objectives and indicators. Ongoing reform efforts focus on streamlining the indicators to make them clearer for parliamentarians and the public. In parallel, building on the work of the "Stiglitz-Sen-Fitoussi" Commission on the Measurement of Economic Performance and Social Progress, France enacted a law in 2015 requiring the government to present wealth and well-being indicators other than GDP when tabling the annual budget, to promote debate on policy impacts. The LOLF performance framework lends itself well to such a presentation; the French authorities are currently planning to implement a strategic dashboard using a limited set of internationally-comparable KNIs on the following three themes:

- Economic development indicators, such as foreign direct investment flows to France (OECD), and "Ease of doing business" (World Bank).
- Social progress indicators, such as healthy life expectancy at 65 by gender (OECD), percentage of 18-24 year-olds with no qualification and who are not in training (France Stratégie/Eurostat), and poverty gaps (World Bank).
- Sustainable development indicators, such as greenhouse gas emissions per unit of GDP (European Energy Agency/Eurostat).

New Zealand Treasury's Living Standards Framework: The mission of the New Zealand Treasury is "to promote better living standards for New Zealanders", and this is interpreted and applied by reference to a "living standards framework". The framework encompasses five broad dimensions grouped under three principal themes (prosperity, inclusiveness and sustainability), which are used systematically as a basis for framing policy advice and evaluation:

Prosperity

- Potential economic growth – Higher incomes, stronger growth and efficient allocation of resources Inclusiveness
- Sustainability for the future – Human and physical capital and sustainability of the environment
- Equity – Distribution across society and opportunities for people to improve their position
- Sustainability
- Social cohesion – Core institutions that underpin society, self-identity, trust and connections
- Resilience – Ability to withstand unexpected systemic shocks

Source: www.stiglitz-sen-fitoussi.fr/.

Building a vision of inclusive growth at all levels of government

A whole-of-government approach at the central government level will have greater potential impact on inclusion if all levels of government are on board.

Many of the policies that have a significant impact on Inclusive growth are managed at least in part by subnational governments. Across the OECD, the almost 134 000 subnational governments are responsible for around 63% of public procurement, 59% of public investment and 40% of total government expenditure.

Subnational governments have important roles in, among other things, enhancing and sustaining skill formation and job creation and retention, the infrastructure that determines travel times and influences pollution emissions, and the services that contribute to the well-being of residents (OECD, 2015a) and (OECD, 2014a). In the area of public investment, for example, the OECD Recommendation on Effective Public Investment across Levels of Government[1] emphasises the importance of vertical co-ordination to achieve impact.[2]

Moreover, policies for inclusive growth will need to take into account the often wide regional variations in conditions and preferences.

For example, high-school drop-outs are often likely to have greater difficulty finding jobs, to have lower incomes and to experience greater health problems. Yet, the roots of high drop-out rates vary according to context: while urban locations have the density of population to provide education in proximity, the quality of education or other social factors may contribute to lack of completion for some students. In a rural area, the problem may in part stem from the lack of critical mass of students to provide education in proximity and long transport times that may hinder school attendance.

Selecting national and regional indicators to tailor policy responses.

Using multidimensional metrics of well-being can help national and local governments to map needs and to design and deliver effective policies, as well as how the benefits of growth, including non-income outcomes, are shared across population groups and places.

Key insights, drawn from international experiences in OECD countries carried out under the aegis of the OECD work on measuring regional well-being (OECD, 2014b), underline the importance of building synergies across policy domains to improve coherence of policies and delivery of results. In particular, while the well-being indicators help to align policies towards shared high-level outcomes, policy makers need a thorough dialogue across different sectors and levels of government and with civil society and the private sector to identify the policy outputs of specific public policies and how these outputs contribute to the final high-level outcomes. Indeed, the OECD has expanded the measures of the economic and quality-of-life factors to the subnational level (Figure 2.3), recognising that the performance of regions and cities should be benchmarked against a variety of dimensions.

Figure 2.3. Regional disparities in life expectancies at birth

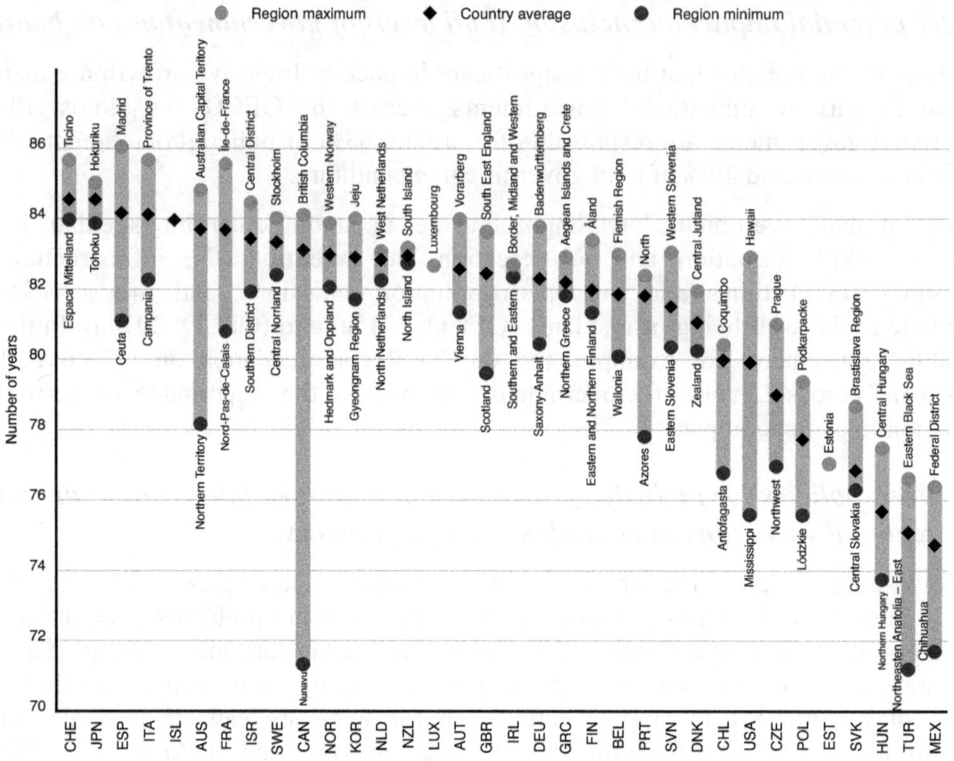

Note: Turkish region TRA2: Agri, Kars,Igdir, Ardahan

Source: OECD (2015), OECD Regional Statistics (database), http://dx.doi.org/10.1787/region-data-en.)

Case studies offer insights into different methodological and political solutions for using well-being metrics in policy making.

Comparative experience offers examples of how indicators can be used in different phases of the policy-making process, such as selecting regional well-being outcome indicators, monitoring progress in people's circumstances over time and implementing a process of multi-stakeholder engagement to promote social change (Box 2.3). In fact, identifying indicators need not be perfect at the earlier stages. Indeed, governments that follow a strategic whole-of-government approach, starting with vision-setting, have often launched their outcomes framework with a number of place holders, and have continued to revise it.[3]

Box 2.3. Using well-being metrics in policy making

The OECD report How's Life in Your Region? Measuring Regional and Local Well-being for Policy Making provides seven in-depth case studies on different methodological and political solutions for using well-being metrics in policy making. In the case of Rome, Italy, a comprehensive consultation process was used to prioritise the dimensions of well-being that matter most to the citizens, through community surveys, a web tool, public meetings, workshops, etc. The region of Sardinia, Italy, made concrete improvements in public service delivery as a result of the effective engagement of public institutions, the private sector and civil society around clear and measurable well-being objectives. For example, the amount of urban waste landfilled was halved and the share of recycled urban waste raised from 27% to 48% over five years. With its Good Life initiative, Southern Denmark included a comprehensive set of regional well-being indicators in its Regional Development Plan, combining objective and perception-based indicators to monitor social progress in the region. The North of the Netherlands developed a sophisticated set of regional well-being indicators by involving various stakeholders, such as the academic community (e.g. University of Groningen). Newcastle, United Kingdom, is a good example of a city that built on national requirements (to establish local health and well-being boards per the 2012 Health and Social Care Act) in order to develop a wide-ranging local well-being strategy. The state of Morelos, Mexico, designed its state development plan around a set of clear baselines and targets in different dimensions of well-being over a pre-determined time frame (corresponding to the state government mandate). Finally, the United States' Partnership for Sustainable Communities is a national initiative for jurisdictions of all sizes. It aims to align federal policies and funding in order to improve access to affordable housing, provide more transport options and reduce transport costs, and protect the environment. The initiative takes stock of existing indicators – identified with the help of focus groups and governmental agencies – and provides guidelines to local policy makers on their use.

Source: OECD (2014b).

Managing trade-offs and shaping actions for impact

Aligning vision and resources: Strategic multi-year budgeting: Building on a shared vision, government strategies and priorities can be identified for both the near and longer terms.

This strategic planning process is typically embodied in a medium-term National Development Plan, Programme for Government or Coalition Agreement, which should reflect high-level outcome targets for the country on the basis of Key National Indicators, as outlined above. Translating these goals into actions requires an alignment between strategic, political planning processes and the resource allocation, service delivery and accountability processes of government.

Good budgeting practices – as outlined in the OECD Recommendation on Budgetary Governance (OECD, 2015b) – have a role to play in different aspects of policy making for inclusive growth.

To begin with, sound budgeting is central to prudent economic management, which should underpin, investment sustained economic growth. Moreover, the budgeting function – perhaps more so than any other function of government – is concerned with making choices and helping governments to identify and weigh multidimensional trade-offs across various strands of public policy that must contend for limited resources.

Indeed, the Recommendation recognises that, for the budget process to work effectively in improving people's lives, it must interconnect with the other dimensions of public governance, including planning at the centre of government, accessibility and openness of government data, and engagement with stakeholders.

Addressing the multidimensional objectives of inclusive growth requires a sustained medium-term effort.

Inclusive growth outcomes, by their nature, typically are visible over a multiyear period (unlike output and activity measures which can be tracked more regularly). A mismatch between the annual resource allocation process and the medium-term Inclusive growth agenda would likely lead to reality falling short of aspirations. Medium-Term Expenditure Frameworks (MTEFs), which serve to increase the visibility of resources over a multi-year period, can be further leveraged to address this challenge and guide the translation of MTEF ceilings into annual allocations of resources, i.e. money and staff. OECD analysis illustrates that most member countries have moved to implement a system of medium-term budgeting: the challenge is to develop an MTEF which has real force in shaping the annual dynamic of the budget cycle, and thus is effective in bridging medium-term planning and in providing the resources needed to deliver on a shared vision (OECD, 2015b).

Apart from the need to ensure consistency between annual allocations and multi-year plans, it is important to assess the impact of the budget decisions on inclusive growth outcomes.

The process of impact assessment should start, but should not end, with an evaluation of the financial impact on the average householder. As discussed above, inclusive growth concerns more than the average citizen: an inclusive growth focus must therefore examine impacts on the wide variety of individuals and groups in society, including those who are marginalised and those minority groups whose position has little in common with national averages. There is also the opportunity to highlight the position of members of society who may be subject to structural, systemic or historical discrimination (e.g. on the basis of gender or ethnicity) to bring transparency to the allocation of resources and to assist in monitoring impacts.

Table 2.1 Including inclusive growth considerations in budget impact assessments

Budget assessment dimension	Description
Household income	Increase/decrease in net take-home financial position across the salary/benefit scale; classified by household type (single, one-parent, two-parent, number of children, number of other dependents, housing status)
Well-being impacts	Effects of budget measures on a range of well-being indicators, such as access to and quality of healthcare; housing status; access to education; cultural and community life
Environmental impacts	Effects and costing of budget measures as to their impact on production of CO2 and/or other environmentally deleterious emissions
Gender impacts	Relative quantified net impacts of budget measures by gender
Ethnic impacts	Relative income and other impacts of budget measures on particular ethnic groups in society
Poverty impacts	Effects of budget measures, including income, material deprivation indicators and other well-being indicators, on the position of underprivileged and/or marginalised sections of the population

Comprehensive, inclusive growth-sensitive budget impact assessments have yet to become a reality.

Although impact assessments could ideally consider each of the dimensions that matter for people's well-being, the full use of this spectrum of assessment criteria is still the exception, rather than the norm, across OECD countries. Nevertheless, some countries have made good progress in addressing some of these dimensions (Table 2.1). For example, Ireland produces a comprehensive assessment of how the annual budget measures affect net household income, with extensive case studies of different representative household types. The budget also includes a poverty impact assessment. In addition, Austria has designed its performance management system to be explicitly responsive to gender issues: each government ministry must include one gender-related objective among its small number of overall key objectives, which in turn form the structural basis for allocating resources and reporting on impacts in the context of the budget.

Ex ante evaluations: The case of government expenditure and regulations

Ex ante evaluation is essential for decision-makers to weigh and design policy interventions.

Across the field of public policy, there has been a long tradition of ex ante appraisal of capital investment, which involves high upfront outlays and has long-term impacts on the development capacity of the economy. Nevertheless, it has been less widely accepted that, in principle, all forms of major expenditure – current as well as capital – should be subject to rigorous ex ante appraisal. Current expenditure programmes, although they may have smaller upfront costs than capital investments, tend to persist for longer, and the lifetime costs can be large. It is for this reason that the OECD Recommendation on Budgetary Governance now includes a call to governments to conduct routine and open ex ante evaluations of all substantive new policy proposals to assess coherence with national priorities, clarity of objectives, and anticipated costs and benefits.

Techniques are available for ex ante analysis of expenditure for inclusive growth.

One of the reasons for the traditional distinction between current and capital programmes, as regards the use of ex ante evaluation, has been the perceived non-applicability of capital appraisal methodologies to current spending. While capital programmes traditionally have a distinct focus on delivering an economic benefit which lends itself to standard calculation (e.g. internal rate of return, net present value), the same has not been the case for current-funded programmes, where results can be more social, intangible and thus (the argument goes) incalculable. In fact, modern public financial management techniques are quite capable of bringing similar analytical rigour to bear on ex ante assessment of current programmes. Techniques such as cost-effectiveness analysis (a standard methodology which allows for identifying trade-offs within a specific sector, such as health care) and multi-criteria analysis permit these complexities to be managed in a way that is useful to decision-makers. The latter technique, in particular, holds the potential to allow for the broad range of public policy dimensions, notably those associated with inclusive growth, to be factored in and weighed as an integral part of the policy formulation process.

Country experiences are instructive.

For example, Ireland has expanded its traditional capital-appraisal methodologies, which originated in large part in the management of European Union-funded programmes, to public expenditure more generally, including current programmes (Box 2.4).

Box 2.4. Towards holistic evaluation of expenditure: Ireland's public spending code

Ireland has a long tradition of robust capital appraisal mechanisms, which were refined in particular in the context of the drawdown and application of European Union regional development funds during the 1980s and 1990s. The ex ante appraisal requirements in respect of capital investments are set out as follows:

1. Define the objective of the proposed expenditure intervention
2. Explore realistic alternative options of achieving the objective – including the option of doing nothing – taking account of constraints including financing, technological capacity and "general policy consideration"
3. Quantify the costs of viable options and specify sources of funding
4. Analyse the main options using standard analytical techniques including financial analysis, cost-benefit analysis, cost-effectiveness analysis, cash-flow analysis and multi-criteria analysis
5. Identify the risks associated with each viable option
6. Decide on and specify a preferred option, including a time profile and financial profile for action
7. Make a recommendation to the decision-making authority, explaining the analytical rationale

Since 2011, these general appraisal requirements have been explicitly extended to all forms of expenditure, current as well as capital, as part of an expanded Public Spending Code. The additional guidance for current funded programmes makes the following specifications:

1. Preparation of a detailed business case incorporating a financial and economic appraisal
2. Provision for a sunset clause, after which the expenditure scheme will be reviewed and discontinued unless it can be demonstrated to meet value-for-money criteria
3. Fixed cash limits for demand-led schemes
4. Pilot implementation of new proposals, where feasible, before final approval is granted
5. "Evaluation-proofing" of all business cases and related memoranda for government, to ensure that performance objectives and criteria defining success and failure are apparent from the outset, and can thus be used in the context of future ex post evaluation

Source: Public Spending Code, http://publicspendingcode.per.gov.ie.

While ex ante assessment of current expenditure programmes has tended to be relatively under-developed in OECD countries, the same does not apply in the area of regulatory policy.

Regulatory impact analysis (RIA) is a tool and a process to inform decision- makers on whether and how to regulate to achieve policy goals. It represents a central element in the regulatory governance cycle, and it is widely adopted to ensure that regulation works effectively and is in the public interest. As a tool supporting decision-making, RIA examines the potential impacts of government actions by focusing on the costs and benefits of a regulatory measure, on the effectiveness of the measure to achieve its policy goals and on whether or not there are superior alternative approaches available to governments. As a decision process, RIA complements consultation initiatives in order (i) to communicate information ex ante about the expected effects of regulatory proposals at a time and in a form that can be used by decision-makers, and (ii) to assist governments ex post to evaluate existing regulations (OECD, 2009).

RIA plays a role in informing policy making for inclusive growth.

By definition, RIA aims to provide information on the distributional impacts of regulation (across groups, sectors, regional areas, etc.), which can help reveal and monitor the trade-offs between the economic, social and environmental effects of potential regulatory responses. The process of developing a RIA is in itself an opportunity to gather the inputs of regulated and more generally of affected parties. Beyond these generic features of RIA, a more focused use of the tool to promote social inclusiveness is also possible through assessing specific impacts. Indeed, recent OECD analysis (OECD, 2015i and 2015d) shows some use by OECD countries of the RIA process to assess the distributional effects of regulation on disadvantaged social groups, gender, poverty and job creation (Figure 9). Spain for instance requires impact assessment on gender and regional distribution and encourages social impact assessment, including on equal opportunity and non-discrimination.[4] However, the assessment of distributional effects generally focuses on large groups, such as government, businesses and communities, without going into specific population sub-groups and without targeting inequality per se. RIA also tends to focus on economic impacts, rather than on more multidimensional effects that are relevant for inclusiveness, and often are conducted too late in the regulatory policy cycle to usefully inform decision-making.

Figure 2.4. Types of impacts integrated into RIA (December 2014)

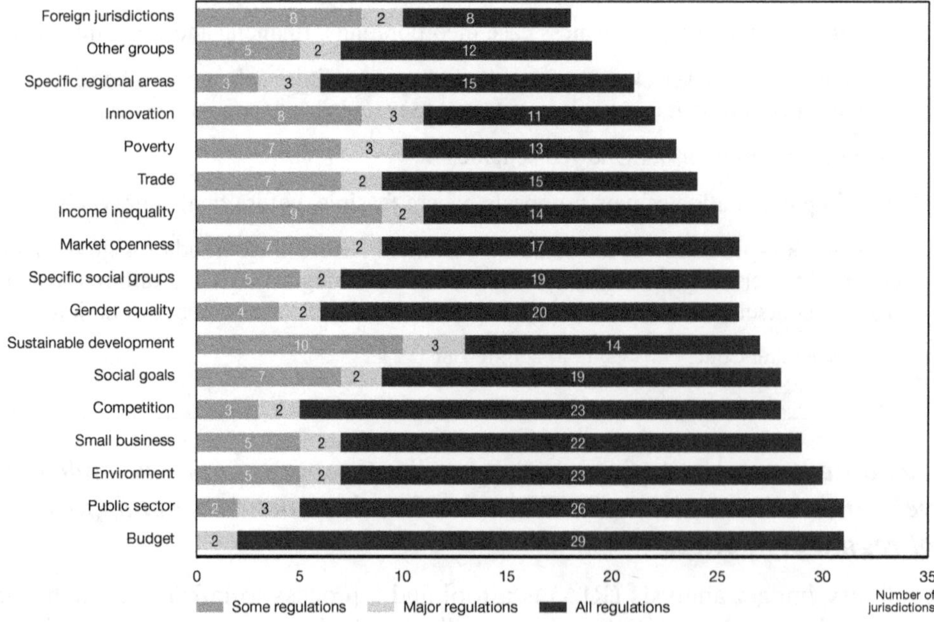

There is much potential for government to clarify what is expected from line ministries in relation to mainstreaming distributional considerations in the RIA process.

For instance, countries could clarify in their RIA guidelines or frameworks which specific types of regulation the assessment of distributional impact is required and which level of analysis is expected (macro versus micro analysis). The guidelines should define how to display this type of impact within the RIA document. For instance, in the United States the RIA guidelines explicitly call for measuring and outlining distributional impacts in a specific section of the RIA document, which helps stakeholders to better focus and consider distributional aspects.

Clarifying the methodology and providing the tools to measure distributional impacts (both quantitatively and qualitatively) would also help to support line ministries in assessing impacts that are mostly qualitative in nature.

A number of countries, including Austria, Switzerland and the United Kingdom, provide guidance and methodology to assess the distributional effects of regulation. In Sweden a manual with guiding questions to be asked on gender equality as part of the assessment process is provided to support regulators. The European Commission guidance for assessing social impacts provides some methodological information on how to assess impacts on employment and the labour market. Furthermore, other technical and capacity challenges need to be addressed, such as gathering information that is relevant for the design of inclusive growth policies; developing standard models and tools to measure social impacts and quantify the qualitative impacts; using a broader range of methodological tools, such as multi-criteria analysis; dealing with a lack of adequate skills and resources within line ministries and regulatory agencies; and mitigating the risk of overloading the RIA procedures.

In parallel with RIA, some countries implement gender impact assessments (GIA) to evaluate the implications of proposed policies, programmes and regulations on men and women.

Requirements for ex ante Gender Impact Assessments of primary legislation are becoming more commonplace among OECD countries (OECD, 2011b). The majority of OECD countries reserve GIAs for primary and secondary legislation rather than for policies and programmes. However, GIAs are most effective if integrated at early stages of the development policies and programmes and sustained through all phases of the policy cycle, including implementation, monitoring and evaluation. Additionally, as suggested in the forthcoming Recommendation on Gender Equality in Public Life, ex ante gender impact assessment needs to be generally aligned with broader policy assessment processes, whether in RIA or expenditure appraisals, in order to be fully anchored within public administrative procedures.

There is much scope to reinforce ex ante evaluation as a standard tool of policy making for inclusive growth. In particular:

- Standardise the common, foundational methodology for ex ante assessment, encompassing both public expenditure and regulatory policy, in order to make policy development simpler and less opaque. Particular attention should be paid to developing standard models for measuring social impacts and gauging the qualitative impacts of policy interventions.

- Develop specialist analytical resources and make them available across government; and overcome institutional and policy silos which prevent a more holistic approach to policy design and re-design. This should go beyond economic tools to encompass sociological expertise for gathering data on social, gender, environmental and other qualitative dimensions.
- Develop data visualisation tools and resources to inform policy choices and trade-offs and to make the policy development cycle more accessible to stakeholders inside and outside of public administration Using Open Government Data to expand policy horizons.

Open government data (OGD) can further strengthen government capacity to define a vision for inclusive growth.

Traditionally, public sector information is created, collected and kept in silos – both from the perspective of organisational culture and technical interoperability. The increased release of OGD means that other stakeholders are able to access and reuse government data in potentially innovative ways that augment the internal analytical capacity within government and increase the visibility of the data across organisational boundaries. Moreover, the open release of data allows for mixing public data with commercial, civil society and citizen input data. It also permits pooling with data produced by other public agencies and/or levels of government – i.e. developing shared content, services and policies between cities or countries; this holds considerable potential for creating public value. Being able to spot trends, evaluate the effectiveness of past and ongoing initiatives, and plan targeted interventions is critical to high-value policy creation. Moreover, OGD can be used to spur public participation and social engagement, as will be discussed in Chapter 3.

Despite progress, much remains to be done.

Authorities across OECD countries point to the need in the future not just for drawing on citizens' inputs and facilitating data analytics, for example to develop and simulate public policies and better target services, but also for a more qualitative approach, including for example ethnographic surveys. Datasets on immigration flows and ethnographies are not available in all countries, whereas their availability as OGD could foster a deeper understanding of the societal needs and support the design and delivery of services that are more inclusive. There is therefore a need for both big quantitative data crunching to provide explicit codified evidence for public sector activities, on the one hand, as well as more qualitative survey data to contextualise big data to provide the necessary implicit and un-codified evidence.

Moreover, countries are still struggling to develop the skills the public sector needs to conduct and make the best use of data analytics and the capacities to reconcile data, privacy and security.

Creating these capacities is essential to spur availability of Open Government Data which can be used and re-used to drive better decisions and better policy development. At the same time, there are legitimate public concerns with regard to privacy and security in the use of big data and the release of OGD. It is important for governments to be vigilant in ensuring that public trust is maintained through high standards of data protection and privacy controls, as well as transparency with citizens as to how governments hold and use personal information. Data protection also encompasses the security of critical information and communication technology (ICT) infrastructure and databases from potential breaches, intentional or accidental.

Promoting government accountability for inclusive growth

Performance-related budgeting processes are particularly relevant for inclusive growth.

While practices vary across countries, the key features of effective performance budgeting systems are identified in the OECD Recommendation on Budgetary Governance. In the context of inclusive growth policy making, it is important that the performance objectives specified in the budget should correspond with the Key National Indicators identified during whole-of-government planning, as discussed above. To the extent that these indicators reflect the requirements of inclusive growth, the entire process of resource allocation will thereby be mobilised and oriented in support of this agenda.

Recent country experiences are instructive.

For example, Austria has in recent years reformed and streamlined its budgetary framework so that each ministry must specify a small number of performance objectives, while the resources allocated to each objective are made explicit in the annual budget document. Likewise, New Zealand has a well-developed results approach, whereby agencies are organised around the outcomes that matter to citizens, and in this context each agency must specify the "vital few" indicators that will tell whether these goals are being achieved. The United States has also placed a high priority on articulating clear performance objectives for each agency, including a small number of "agency priority goals"; these objectives have become an organising principle for public accountability and also for internal management and staff engagement. Scotland's National Performance Framework involves a co-ordination mechanism to ensure alignment of strategies and programmes across sectors, in support of broader national outcomes.[5]

The availability of comparable, timely and usable information will become increasingly important.

It is likely that, together with traditional performance-tracking mechanisms, Open Government Data will be used more and more to complement performance indicators on public policy outcomes and quality of services, helping policy makers to shed light on inefficiencies but also to compare the performance of different providers of public services (e.g. public schools and hospitals). For example, OGD can (i) facilitate benchmarking across government services and identify opportunities for improving the delivery of financial and social benefits/impacts; (ii) help government make savings by automatically tracking prices paid through public contracts; and (iii) help identify gaps in the data that can be used to fully capture all aspects relevant to assess public sector performance. Indeed, a few OECD governments are currently maximising the value of OGD to complement performance indicators, including the United Kingdom, which uses OGD to assess performance of hospitals (OECD, 2015e).

Aligning incentives and horizontal co-ordination

Public performance is naturally dependent on the quality, capability and motivation of public servants, which is particularly challenging in the context of inclusive growth.

Performance management and performance-based arrangements for senior civil servants (SCSs) exist in most OECD member and non-member countries. However, in the context of inclusive growth, as responsibility lies across ministerial lines, the challenge becomes one of not only aligning SCS performance goals with ministerial expectations, but also incentivising co-operation and co-ordination across institutional silos. One way to do this can be to align incentives with projects that are horizontal in nature. The Canadian province of Alberta has done this with senior civil servants' performance-related pay (Box 2.5).

Box 2.5. Building incentives for agility and collaboration in Alberta, Canada

In Alberta, Canada, officials agreed that getting departments to work together is the biggest challenge to public service and that achieving this depends on the behaviours of senior officials in the departments. The most effective incentive to joining up has been to explicitly link the performance pay of senior officials to horizontal policy initiatives. For deputy ministers, the heads of the departments, 20% of their remuneration package is based on performance, and 75% of this is based on their performance in horizontal issues. For assistant deputy ministers, 50% of their performance pay is based on horizontal initiatives. This has created a meaningful incentive to focus on the success of the government's horizontal initiatives, even if it requires re-allocating resources away from achieving the goals in the department's business plan.

Source: Määtä (2011).

In parallel with aligning performance assessment frameworks, the capacities and skills needed to design, implement and assess inclusive growth policies should be reconsidered.

The multidimensional nature of inclusive growth outcomes calls for reinforcing the capacities of public servants to contribute to a whole-of-government view of interlinked and complex policy challenges. Indeed, OECD countries share a common challenge of developing their workforces in ways that reinforce mobility and cut through organisational silos. Greater mobility within the public workforce can help to foster a corporate, whole-of-government perspective on new challenges posed by inclusive growth. Mobility can also facilitate attraction and retention, as varied job experiences are often attractive to applicants and can keep employees motivated. Baseline conditions required to enable internal mobility are uniform employment and pay terms and conditions. Once these are established, organisations often develop and use secondment policies and other mobility programmes to provide fixed-term assignments to other organisations, thereby simultaneously building the experience of the workforce and promoting sharing across organisational boundaries.

A horizontal challenge such as inclusive growth needs a public sector workforce ready to think across organizational lines. Mobility helps.

Country experiences offer insights on human resource management for inclusive growth.

Some OECD governments establish specific job rotation programmes within organisations or across ministries. Due to the management challenges of such programmes, enrolement is usually limited to employees who stand out in terms of development potential and to specific cadres of managers. These programmes sometimes establish upward mobility. Additionally, many public services see time spent in other agencies or the centre of government as a prerequisite for advancing to higher levels of management and leadership. This can ensure that senior leaders are aware of the work of other organisations and consider issues that extend beyond their own sphere of direct control. Moreover, leadership training programmes offer a valuable way to impart whole-of-government perspectives to mid- and senior-level managers, especially when they are run centrally and organised around horizontal leadership principles such as innovation.[6] Indeed, recent OECD work on human resource management tools to support more public sector innovation has highlighted a range of practices that encourage and reward successful collaboration across organisations. These include developing and maintaining networks, formal and informal, at all levels of government, as well as using awards processes to collect successful innovative practices and share them across the civil service.

Making service delivery more inclusive

Improving access and reach

Inclusive growth relies on the effective, efficient delivery of public services to citizens.

As outlined in Chapter 1, access to quality services, such as education, health care and justice is essential to break ingrained cycles of disadvantage, and to allow for marginalised groups to benefit from higher-paid jobs, better living standards and longer, more fulfilling lives.[7] Further, developing human capital is at the heart of the transmission mechanism through which income inequality may be detrimental to economic growth. The reverse is true as well: higher educational attainment and better skills is one of the strongest drivers of economic growth in the long run and can at the same time offset at least in part rising earnings inequality (OECD, 2015f).

Higher educational attainment and better skills is one of the strongest drivers of economic growth and can help offset earnings inequality.

Inequalities in access to services persist today in OECD countries in part due to increasing complexities in delivering quality services and expanding access.

Governments must respond to increasing quality and efficiency expectations, as well as address demographic changes and pressures to consolidate public finances. Within many OECD countries[8] societies are becoming more diverse, the urban-rural divide continues to widen, and there can be large discrepancies in income and access to services within cities. Moreover, service delivery models are changing, calling for an innovative, systematic and consistent approach to ensure public sector productivity, particularly in the cost-intensive welfare service delivery areas. The combined potential of digital transformation, innovation and updated skills of the public sector can help governments reduce the fixed costs of service delivery, while improving the quality, reach and targeting of services.

Leveraging access to services for inclusive growth implies first and foremost understanding where and what the needs are.

Understanding the challenges associated with access begins with information, such as the number and location of service institutions, their geographical features, user feedback, transportation network and economic cost. These differences are policy-relevant because they reflect the opportunities available to people and the extent of inequality, including in terms of territorial disparities. A number of mechanisms can be used to better map demand and tailor service provision, including digital technologies (such as geo-localisation and real-time feedback through social media), user experience feedback and new forms of service delivery.

Knowing citizen needs is key to meeting them. Tools are available that help policy makers better map demand and tailor service provision.

Understanding user needs and experiences allows governments to tailor services provision and improve access, including for disadvantaged groups.

The solution to many contemporary societal challenges is not necessarily more public services, but rather better targeted, better designed services, that improve access for the most hard-to-reach users.[9] The traditional model of service provision, based on individual administrative transactions, should be replaced with whole-of-government solutions, recognising the need to make users part of the design of relevant services. An example of this is the "life-cycle approach" or "user's journey" introduced in some OECD countries as a mean to increase access (in terms of reduced complexity) to service users but also satisfaction and a more effective use of public resources (Box 2.6). Other examples come from the justice sector, where countries are exploring innovative ways to address the diverse legal needs of citizens and remove barriers to access, especially for the disadvantaged groups. Strategies range from enhancing the use of technology, such as mobile applications for accessing legal services, to targeting legal aid services to respond to citizen's personal circumstances. Some countries are also developing options for better case triage and better client orientation with links to other services (health or social) and establishing a "no wrong door" approach (e.g. justice one-stop shops). To improve access in remote areas, some countries offer tailored dispute resolution services, decentralise courts and enhance provision of public legal services in rural areas.

Box 2.6. Life events approach to service delivery

The "life events" or "user's journey" approach designs service delivery around the key life events of a user and provides a framework for the government to collect evidence that services are delivered in an effective and fair manner from the user's point of view. First, the key life events of a typical user are selected (e.g. giving birth, graduating from university, or starting up a business). Second, a representative survey identifies how many users have recently experienced a particular life event and how many of them find administrative steps related to this life event complicated (fair, inclusive, etc.). Third, a focus group of users who recently experienced a particular life event goes through a "customer journey mapping" to identify the concrete bottlenecks in service delivery.

Box 2.6. Life events approach to service delivery *(continued)*

This approach helps governments to focus resources on the most problematic areas of service delivery, and improve transparency and accountability, especially when done repeatedly. The life events methodology also has the potential to improve service delivery for disadvantaged groups. In France, for example, this approach has been used to study administrative barriers to recent immigrants. Using the methodology, administrative procedures related to the life event "I am an immigrant (non-EU national)" have been found the most complex of all life events studied. Disabled groups have also been identified as constrained by bureaucracy. Results showed that administrative procedures related to the life event "I'm disabled/one of my close relatives is disabled" are severely complex, which has helped the government to understand the administrative customer's journey of these disadvantaged groups.

Taking a "life events" approach to understanding service delivery provides a comprehensive framework for mapping citizen service needs.

Collaboration between service users, service providers and professionals can also lead to public services that are better designed and delivered in partnership with citizens (Box 2.7).

In such a scheme, citizens/users are invited to participate in the whole process of service delivery, which can improve outcomes through community involvement and tackle service failures (OECD, 2011c). Such approaches draw on the unique knowledge and resources of service users, resulting in more customised service delivery for more effective results. The public administration acts as a facilitator or convener, recognising the assets that citizens have and bringing them into the delivery equation (Box 2.7). The role of voluntary and community organisations is often critical, particularly in targeting those most in need, and helping to implement services effectively.

Box 2.7. Co-producing better health outcomes

Governments must respond to the challenge of longer life expectancy and re-orient services towards preventing ill health, rather than just responding to illness. In transforming services, users become key partners to deliver desired outcomes and reduce the costs of expensive, acute health services or residential care. A variety of approaches can be used in co-producing better health outcomes. A combination of home-based technology, self-management by service users and targeted professional support can enable patients to manage their own care on a day-to-day basis, while relying on expert service for specialised or complex functions and as back up. Potentially, this can release resources either to reduce levels of public spending or for transfer to other priorities. Training service users to be a source of information and support for others with the same conditions allows patients to take more control over their health while helping others. This scheme combines elements of co-production with individuals and community, as it makes expertise available to other groups of patients and builds support networks. These approaches share an emphasis on prevention and may reduce the need for expensive services, such as emergency hospital admissions or outpatient visits. By doing so, user co-production can reduce costs to the public purse also potentially improve health services.

Box 2.7. Co-producing better health outcomes *(continued)*

Evaluations of these approaches in countries like the Netherlands, the United Kingdom or the United States have shown their positive impact not only in terms of cost efficiency (for example, by reducing visits to the emergency room) but also in secondary outcomes, including well-being and satisfaction. There are also potential savings for future expenditure, which are more difficult to quantify and which will result from better management of ongoing conditions.

Source: OECD (2011c).

Citizen input makes a difference. Citizens have unsurpassed knowledge of their own needs. How can policy makers tap into this knowledge to better design services?

Social investment, social impact bonds and associated outcomes funds are other examples of policy instruments that can be used to improve provision, focus on outcomes and cut across administrative silos.

Social impact bonds were first launched in the United Kingdom and offer an innovative way to finance solutions to social issues. A social impact bond is a type of public-private partnership that embeds a pay-for-success scheme, commissioned by public authorities, foundations or corporations to provide social goods and services. These public-private partnership models, when implemented in a context of transparency and accountability, can contribute to much needed innovation in financing models as well as improvement in public service delivery (OECD, 2015g).

Increasing services inclusiveness through digital welfare Digitisation can affect a range of public services in the social area.

Digitisation can affect a range of public services in the social area.

In education, technology is enabling new teaching and learning methods, as well as new mechanisms to facilitate administration, parent interaction, and teacher-pupil and pupil-pupil relations. In the area of health, new service models are also emerging (Box 2.8). Patients have better access to information, which leads to their increased independence and empowerment in care. Digitisation will play a key role to leverage this transformation in public welfare areas given its potential to increase productivity and inclusiveness of service production and delivery. In the short term, this digitisation will be a precondition for ensuring sound fiscal policies. In the longer run, it will be equally important to maintain the public sector's credibility in terms of efficient and effective service delivery responsive to users' needs, thus nurturing public trust in governments' capacity to boost more inclusive processes and growth (OECD, 2016 forthcoming). Only by addressing these issues – and related themes such as new ethical challenges, building local commitment and ownership, and ensuring that groups are not left behind by digital welfare initiatives – will more countries embrace the potential of digitisation as a strategic model for service delivery.

Leveraging digitisation in transforming public welfare areas can increase the productivity and inclusiveness of service production and delivery.

Building capacity for new forms of service delivery.

Digitisation and new forms of service production and delivery imply a shift towards a multi-stakeholder, demand-driven strategy, calling for new skills and accountability models in the public sector (OECD, 2015i).

Addressing the required cultural change and preparing public sector staff for new professional roles – as stewards or commissioners rather than producers – implies investing in new knowledge and skills, such as behavioural insights, design thinking and digital skills such as social media management. Some government institutions have taken up the challenge of developing a new set of skills and capacities. For example, the Australian Public Service has a systematic approach to developing skills for digital government reforms, which was recently adapted to include ICT, social media and collaborative approaches, including for service delivery (Mickoleit, 2014). Similarly, the UK Government created Policy Lab in 2014 to identify and test new tools and techniques for policy making, including design, digital and data. The government has shared these with over 1 500 policy makers to date.

Box 2.8. Denmark's strategy for improved service delivery: digital welfare and open government data

Continuing the last decade of achievements in digital government, in 2011 the Danish Government and the representatives of the regions and the municipalities agreed on The Digital Path to Future Welfare – eGovernment Strategy 2011-2015 (www.digst.dk). This strategy covers 12 focus areas, which include sharing core data for all authorities. The aim is to maximise the power of data and technology to deliver more efficient and inclusive services. The digital strategy outlines three overall milestones regarding data sharing:

- High-quality and cohesive core data ensures that the authorities can serve citizens and companies quickly and easily.
- All authorities reuse core data so that citizens and companies do not have to enter or look for the same data several times.
- Core data is distributed more smoothly, efficiently and reliably thanks to a shared infrastructure for data distribution.

While rather general, these milestones are highly ambitious in terms of full deployment across all parts of the public sector. Following up with further analysis, the strategy includes specific actionable commitments such as budgetary consequences through the annual budget agreements between the central government, the regions and the municipalities. Together with the Annual Government Budget Act, these budget agreements provide the essential strategic orientations and define the overall business case of the Open Government Data initiatives covered.

Source: OECD (2015h).

Setting ambitious digital objectives pays off. Denmark is making important strides in maximising the power of data and technology towards more efficient and inclusive services.

In addition, private sector provision affects citizens' expectations about the services provided by government, specifically with regard to digital services.

If governments cannot provide digital services of the quality and responsiveness that citizens have come to expect from commercial or even non-profit providers, this can ultimately erode trust in the public sector. This is particularly true among the younger generation of "digital natives" who have come to expect a "digital first" approach to any service interactions.

To meet rising expectations of access and quality in a rapidly evolving context, governments should invest in a well-targeted framework for inclusive service delivery.

Within such a framework, governments can align an inclusive growth vision with the means to deliver on it, through shared outcomes accompanied by an actionable set of goals and targets that can be used to monitor implementation (Box 2.9).

A framework for inclusive service delivery helps to align tools and processes towards improving the access and reach of services.

Box 2.9. Integrated service delivery in New Zealand

New Zealand is aiming to deliver better results and improved services to its citizens. To address future challenges, the administration recently started to centre its approach to policy making on citizens rather than on agency.

In this reform, the government acknowledges the council role of ICT. The government created the position of ICT functional leader, a senior public official responsible for creating a single and coherent ICT eco-system that helps deliver smarter, customer-centred services. In addition, the new website Govt.nz (based on Gov.uk) was launched and the following principles adopted for the online service delivery: be user-centred, start small and iterate, try to deliver a more consistent user experience, use plain English and be device-friendly and accessible. New Zealand's experience confirmed the need to listen to users. For example, the first version of Govt.nz was too complicated for users with a limited literacy rate, and changes had to be made.

As a measure of success of the integrated service delivery reform, the government of New Zealand set the following indicators: agencies are collaborating; agencies are using common capabilities; significant savings across the system are being made; assurance frameworks are in place; privacy expectations and standards are set.

Source: OECD analysis based on MacDonald (2015).

In addition, user involvement has to start much earlier than during the evaluation phase of the services.

Effective involvement for the delivery of more inclusive services starts with identifying key issues and collaboratively designing services. But translating these practices into digital service transformation is only emerging across the OECD, and few countries have been able to systematically overhaul the way digital services are conceived and implemented. The work carried out under the guidance of the UK Cabinet Office in recent years is ground-breaking, as it has resulted in new standards for usability of digital services in the form of the public service portal www.gov.uk. To ensure a harmonised public service experience, the Government Digital Service (GDS) has authority to review any digital service against a set of minimum criteria before it can be launched. The GDS also provides assistance to institutions on how to achieve the high standards of quality and user involvement outlined in the Government Service Design Manual22 (OECD, 2015j).

Are you preparing for tomorrow's seamless digital government services? There is plenty of scope to create an outstanding user experience across the full range of digital government services while expanding access and read.

Finally, governments need to be able to measure outcomes and impact on various types of social and economic groups beyond the average.

This will require rethinking many service delivery processes and will put more emphasis on the administration's ability to measure properly the achieved outcomes, including their distribution across different segments of the population and across place-based considerations. Moreover, civil servants will need to be able to engage users in evaluation and service design, which will generate demand for new skills, such as communication and leadership.

Closing the policy cycle: evaluation, accountability and learning

Evaluating the impacts of government expenditure and regulations

While countries have struggled to develop ex ante appraisal methodologies for current spending, this has in general been counter-balanced by a stronger focus on ex post evaluation of such programmes.

The OECD Recommendation on Budgetary Governance details how evaluative mechanisms should be integrated within the budget process – both annual and multi-annual – to ensure that lessons are learned from how well (or poorly) results are being achieved. It underlines that these findings can inform future policy design. The principal expenditure evaluation mechanisms relevant to the inclusive growth (IG) agenda are outlined below (Table 2.2).

Table 2.2. Ex post evaluation of inclusive growth policies

Expenditure evaluation mechanism	Description
Performance (or value for money -VFM) audit	Targeted review, typically carried out by an internal or external audit institution, to assess whether programme objectives are being achieved, and with what levels of efficiency.
Programme evaluation	In-depth evaluation of a specific programme, by reference to original rationale, ongoing relevance, effectiveness in achieving objectives, cost of delivery, alternative modalities and savings/efficiency options. Typically intended to form part of multi- year government-wide expenditure evaluation cycle.
Focused policy assessment	Short, sharp evaluation focused on one or more of the key criteria used in programme evaluation. Typically intended as an element of a time-bound spending review. Could also be used in IG-proofing of programmes.
Spending review	Large-scale re-assessment of the disposition of resources within an entire sector of public expenditure, by reference to new priorities and effectiveness in meeting objectives. Typically used on a periodic basis to identify "fiscal space" for new priorities within the sector.
Comprehensive spending review	Whole-of-government re-assessment of the use of resources across all sectors of public expenditure by reference to new priorities and effectiveness in meeting objectives. Typically used on a periodic basis to identify "fiscal space" for high-level political priorities. Maybe used to assess inclusive growth alignment and expenditure impact.

Ex post evaluations of inclusive growth policies involve a variety of government agencies and public institutions.

The institutions involved in these evaluations range from the line ministries (for internal management purposes and to assist in prioritising within their limited resources), the ministry of finance (to assist in its task of providing the government with options as to resource allocation), the centre of government (in connection with co-ordination of political priorities), and the supreme audit institution (in its primary tasks of facilitating accountability and its "value-added" tasks of improving the quality of administrative, political and public debate about resource allocation) as well as parliaments (to which supreme audit institutions often report and which have a role in evaluating public policies and holding the executive to account for results). It is also open to governments to involve external experts for their input regarding issues of efficiency and performance.

More generally, the evaluation process lends itself particularly well to the task of reassessing and calibrating the government's actions on inclusive growth.

Spending reviews, whether comprehensive or sectorial, provide an ideal opportunity to take stock of how high-level outcome objectives are being advanced. A primary task of such spending reviews is to identify "fiscal space" for spending on new government priorities. These reviews have become a standard part of the budgetary toolkit across most OECD countries. A test of the effectiveness of the inclusive growth agenda over the coming years will be whether governments explicitly recognise inclusive growth as a factor in their evaluation criteria.

Ex post evaluation of large expenditure programmes is particularly pertinent.

This is especially true for public social spending, which is worth 22% of GDP on average across the OECD. In Chile, for example, a number of initiatives have been considered to strengthen ex post evaluation of public programmes, including in the

Ministry of Social Development and the Education Quality Agency; discussions on the need to create an Agency for the Evaluation of Public Policies are ongoing (OECD, 2014c). In the United Kingdom, cost-benefit analysis includes ex post evaluation of public expenditures. Benefits are defined as increases in human well-being (utility), and the trade-offs involved in choosing among different policy options are clearly identified. In that respect, the United Kingdom has one of the most solid traditions in project appraisal to select investments under budget constraints, and ex post expenditure evaluation is perceived as a key policy learning tool (OECD, 2015k).

It is increasingly accepted that inclusive growth requires effective analysis and intervention throughout the regulatory policy cycle.

Therefore, RIA, the traditional tool of ex ante evaluation, needs to be supplemented with greater use of ex post evaluation (as to whether the intended objectives of regulation have been achieved). According to a recent OECD survey (OECD, 2015l), in the last three years, only seven countries have undertaken ex post evaluations frequently for both primary and subordinate legislation. The majority of ex post evaluations that have been conducted in OECD countries over the last 12 years have been of a principle-based nature and not on a specific sector or policy themes. These evaluations have largely focused on reducing the administrative burden. While this represents a useful start, ex post evaluation practices need to expand to assess economic and societal outcomes of policies more broadly. Similarly, while OECD governments undertake Gender Impact Assessments (GIA) across a range of sectors, such as health, labour and finance, to address the gendered nature of policies, programmes and practices, GIAs are yet to become routine elements of policy making. Similar to RIA, the primary focus has been on ex ante assessments, while the practice of ex post gender impact evaluations is rare and would need to be expanded, also in accordance with the forthcoming Recommendation on Gender Equality in Public Life.

Ex post evaluation shouldn't be an afterthought. Their use needs to expand in order to assess economic and societal outcomes of policies across different social groups.

Test your evaluation culture. Check out the themes listed below to see how they can be adapted to your ex post evaluation methodology.

Deepening the culture of evaluation

Strengthening already-established evaluative techniques and broadening their reach within policy dimensions – social as well as economic – is an essential aspect of a strategic policy cycle geared towards inclusive growth.

These processes are essential for assessing policies and re-directing them for optimum impact. They should therefore move beyond their conventional narrow perception as technical mechanisms that are incidental to the thrust of policy design.

A number of elements can help embed and deepen a culture of holistic evaluation.

Such an integrated approach to evaluation, which reflects social as well as economic impacts, could draw from the following themes reflected in various OECD public governance instruments:

- A routine requirement that all public policies be subject to ex ante assessment, whether in the form of a RIA or expenditure appraisal, as outlined above.
- A standardised and publicly-recognised methodology for conducting and presenting these evaluative findings in a way that is accessible to policy makers and non-specialist observers.
- The development of a cadre/community of evaluation professionals within the public service, available to all policy-making agencies, working closely and directly with policy practitioners more broadly, and with supporting feedback loops into the policy processes of government.
- An expectation that government policies, particularly those addressing social outcomes, be subject to routine ex post evaluation. After allowing appropriate space for the internal deliberative processes of government to proceed as normal, results should be made available directly for public scrutiny, so that a constructive debate can be promoted within society at large.

An open, transparent approach to using evidence in public policy can also open the way for the broad range of public institutions to contribute, in a constructive and critical manner, to elaborating policy.

For example, supreme audit institutions have the potential to move beyond their traditional role of financial probity, towards a more substantive engagement on the quality, efficacy and value-for-money of public policy interventions. The clear analytical and accountability focus of the audit function has the power to challenge and strengthen the "programme logic models" that underlie inclusive growth policies, in both their economic and social aspects. Finally, it is parliaments that are ultimately responsible, as representatives of the people, for approving primary legislation and budgets. Greater transparency and openness regarding policy objectives and public performance can also allow parliaments to contribute more actively in assessing laws and spending programmes ex post and linking results of implemented laws to the production of new laws and programmes.

Towards better policy making for inclusive growth

Action on inclusive growth begins with whole-of-government vision and outcome objectives that cut across administrative boundaries to reflect national and political aspirations, a natural role for the centre of government.

The experience of advanced countries in articulating the Key National Indicators that shape a broad, multidimensional national vision shows that it is possible to map and monitor their progress in achieving inclusive growth. Regional well-being indicators are also well-developed across the OECD and provide additional specificity about the targets, impacts and distribution of inclusive growth policies. Likewise, Open Government Data can be leveraged to map trends and present a fuller picture of inclusive growth targets and outcomes.

Strategic alignment of vision and government tools and processes across the policy cycle is essential for delivering on joined outcomes.

Translating inclusive growth goals into reality requires carefully selecting specific policy interventions based on evidence and aligning high-level goals onto budgetary allocations and other policy interventions. Some countries and jurisdictions are already moving towards "outcomes-based national frameworks" (e.g. France, New Zealand and Scotland). Further emphasis should be placed on better understanding the crafting of such frameworks and their implications in terms of consultation, engagement, delivery and accountability.

To assist in evidence-based policy making for inclusive growth, there is scope for developing and applying a common, foundational methodology for evaluation and for emphasising the role of distributional analysis and qualitative techniques.

Systematic assessment and refinement of inclusive growth policies requires that a culture of evaluation and evidence be embedded throughout the public service, drawing on all institutional resources, so that a full economic and social balance sheet can be brought before policy makers and stakeholders. Ex ante policy evaluation is a well-established feature of capital investment policies and of regulatory policy and should be extended to current expenditure interventions. Likewise, regulatory impact assessment (RIA) could assist further by expanding its distributional analysis and including relevant multidimensional impacts, as well as building policy feedback loops earlier in the policy-making process. Whole-of-government accountability systems – with regard to budget allocations, human resource management and programme delivery – can align policy sectors and units towards joined-up delivery by providing incentives for horizontal co-ordination. The strategic policy cycle must embrace ex post evaluation and learning with a focus on multidimensional impact and distribution across social groups.

Whole-of-government accountability systems can align policy sectors and units towards joined-up delivery by providing incentives for horizontal co-ordination.

As a prior step, and apart from necessary alignment of planning and budgeting systems, the budget process itself should be more transparent about the range of inclusive growth impacts arising from budget decisions.

The budget process – in its annual and multi-annual aspects – is fundamentally important in keeping economic growth on course and in resourcing inclusive growth priorities. Impact analysis should go beyond basic income distribution to include impacts on well-being and on vulnerable, marginalised and under-represented groups. Performance budgeting is the natural vehicle for highlighting the objectives of budget policies, organisational objectives and their coherence with overall inclusive growth goals. In addition, medium-term expenditure frameworks (MTEFs), where inclusive growth goals are made manifest, can be further reinforced to bridge medium-term priorities and annual resource allocation.

There are several options for mitigating service access problems, including consolidation of services, co-locating services or merging similar services.

Inclusive growth impacts rely most directly on efficient, targeted public service delivery.

Access and reach of services can be further pursued through innovation, co-creation and alternative service delivery. Policy options include exploring strategies that can mitigate access problems, for example consolidating, co-locating or merging similar services; encouraging the direct involvement of individual users and groups of citizens in planning and delivering public services; and innovation and alternative delivery mechanisms, such as digital welfare, shared services centres or cloud computing.

Public performance itself is critically dependent on the skills, motivation and engagement of staff in the public sector.

To achieve inclusive growth goals, where responsibility can span different agencies, performance management frameworks should incentivise co-operation across institutional silos. Moreover, the skills and capacities of public servants will increasingly need to adapt to the requirements of multi-faceted, government-wide policy design and delivery. In tandem, new capacities for data analytics, data security and new professional roles in the commissioning and oversight of service delivery are needed.

Performance management frameworks should incentivise co-operation across institutional silos and prepare new capacities for data analytics and data security.

In each of these areas, the OECD has a key role to play in facilitating critical discussion among national experts, and in developing tools that underpin international best practice and lay the groundwork for future progress.

While many elements of the inclusive growth agenda are in place, more need to be developed. The overarching work of forging a common framework – bringing all elements together as instruments of modern public governance – remains a key priority for the coming years.

Notes

1 For further information, see www.oecd.org/effective-public-investment-toolkit/.

2 For OECD work on multilevel governance, see www.oecd.org/gov/regional-policy/multi-levelgovernance.htm.

3 For example, Scotland identified where indicators were not available at the time, leaving a placeholder for future development. New Zealand reached out externally to

complement available indicators and also identified those unable to ensure a realistic framework. France is currently embarked in a process of continuous improving their KNIs, to achieve a simpler, more accessible framework.

4 Regulated by Royal Decree 1083/2009.

5 For more information, see www.gov.scot/About/Performance/scotPerforms.

6 Programmes of this kind are increasingly common in OECD countries and benefit leaders in two ways. Leaders are exposed to ideas and insights from the curricula and the sharing of experiences by participants. This, in turn, enables the creation of networks that can be leveraged to stimulate horizontal information sharing and collaboration. In Belgium, for example, the Vitruvius programme, an in-depth 24-day programme conducted over 8 months, has now coached over 450 middle and top leaders.

7 For example, across 15 OECD countries, people with better education live on average 6 years longer at age 30 than people with the lowest level of education. Access to quality health care may explain some of this inequality. Also, there is a strong positive correlation between educational attainment and subjective life satisfaction across countries (Atkinson, 2013). Being born in a disadvantaged family has an impact on a students' performance and access to tertiary education, which, in turn, has an impact on earnings, employment status and also on life expectancy (OECD, 2010).

8 On average, across OECD countries 15% of the variation in students' performance in mathematics can be explained by their socio-economic background. In 2013, more than 50% of students enrolled in tertiary education had at least one parent with that level of education whereas only 10% of children whose parents had not completed their secondary education were enrolled in university. While the majority of OECD countries have achieved and maintained universal coverage for health care, challenges remain. On average across EU countries, people with low incomes are eight times more likely to report unmet care needs. Differences in access remain for spatial reasons (see OECD, 2015k) and access to justice.

9 For further reference, see OECD, 2015m.

References

Atkinson (2015), Inequality, What Can Be Done?, Harvard University Press. Cambridge, Massachusetts. Baena Olabe, P. and J. Cruz Vieyra (2011), Access to Information and Targeted Transparency Policies, IDB-TN-321, Inter-American Development Bank, Washington, DC.

OECD (2015a), *Subnational Governments in OECD Countries: Key Data* (brochure), OECD, Paris, http://dx.doi.org/10.1787/region-data-en.

OECD (2015b), "OECD Recommendation of the Council on Budgetary Governance", [C(2015)1], OECD, Paris.

OECD (2015c), "Promoting inclusive growth through better regulation: The role of regulatory impact assessment", GOV/RPC(2015)4, OECD, Paris.

OECD (2015d), "Using regulatory impact analysis to foster inclusive growth: An expert perspective", GOV/RPC/RD(2015)3, OECD, Paris.

OECD (2015e), Open Government Data Review of Poland: Unlocking the Value of Government Data, OECD Digital Government Studies, OECD Publishing, Paris, http://dx.doi.org/10.1787/9789264241787-en.

OECD (2015f), *In It Together: Why Less Inequality Benefits All*, OECD Publishing, Paris, http://dx.doi.org/10.1787/9789264235120-en.

OECD (2015g), *Social Impact Investment: Building the Evidence Base*, OECD Publishing, Paris, http://dx.doi.org/10.1787/9789264233430-en.

OECD (2016 forthcoming) – Digital Government Strategies for Transforming Public Services in Welfare Areas, OECD Comparative Study, forthcoming.

OECD (2015i), *Slovak Republic: Better Co-ordination for Better.Policies, Services and Results*, OECD Public Governance Reviews, OECD Publishing, Paris, http://dx.doi.org/10.1787/9789264247635-en.

OECD (2015j), "Estonia and Finland: Fostering strategic capacity across governments and digital services across borders", OECD Public Governance Reviews, OECD Publishing, Paris, http://dx.doi.org/10.1787/9789264229334-en.

OECD (2015k), *Government at a Glance 2015*, OECD Publishing, Paris, http://dx.doi.org/10.1787/gov_glance-2015-en.

OECD (2015l), *OECD Regulatory Policy Outlook 2015*, OECD Publishing, Paris, http://dx.doi.org/10.1787/9789264238770-en.

OECD (2015m), *Integrating Social Services for Vulnerable Groups: Bridging Sectors for Better Service Delivery*, OECD Publishing, Paris, http://dx.doi.org/10.1787/9789264233775-en.

OECD (2014a), *OECD Regional Outlook 2014: Regions and Cities: Where Policies and People Meet*, OECD Publishing, Paris, http://dx.doi.org/10.1787/9789264201415-en.

OECD (2014b), *How's Life in Your Region?: Measuring Regional and Local Well-being for Policy Making*, OECD Publishing, Paris, http://dx.doi.org/10.1787/9789264217416-en.

OECD (2014c), *Chile's Supreme Audit Institution: Enhancing Strategic Agility and Public Trust*, OECD Public Governance Reviews, OECD Publishing, Paris, http://dx.doi.org/10.1787/9789264207561-en

OECD (2013), *How's Life? 2013: Measuring Well-being*, OECD Publishing, Paris, http://dx.doi.org/10.1787/9789264201392-en

OECD (2011a), *How's Life?: Measuring Well-being*, OECD Publishing, Paris, http://dx.doi.org/10.1787/9789264121164-en

OECD (2011b), Survey on National Gender Frameworks, Gender Public Policies and Leadership.

OECD (2011c), *Together for Better Public Services: Partnering with Citizens and Civil Society*, OECD Public Governance Reviews, OECD Publishing, Paris, http://dx.doi.org/10.1787/9789264118843-en.

OECD (2010), *Making Reform Happen: Lessons from OECD Countries*, OECD Publishing, Paris, http://dx.doi.org/10.1787/9789264086296-en.

OECD (2009), *Regulatory Impact Analysis: A Tool for Policy Coherence*, OECD Publishing, Paris, http://dx.doi.org/10.1787/9789264067110-en.

Chapter 3.

Shaping policies for inclusive growth: voice, inclusion and engagement

To develop policies that promote Inclusive Growth, public institutions must themselves be inclusive. Governments should give voice to stakeholders and encourage them to engage in decision-making. This chapter describes ways to involve the elderly, youth, unemployed and unprivileged segments of the population. It also focuses on preventing policy capture by special interest groups. The authors address stakeholder engagement in shaping policies, for example through participative budgeting. They describe leveraging tools for engagement, examining access to information and the role of new technologies such Open Government Data and social media. Related challenges are presented, as are various policy levers to involve stakeholders. The chapter also presents ways to ensure that the public sector workforce be inclusive, such as fostering gender equality.

Shaping outcomes that matter most

Efforts to promote inclusive growth must be anchored in an enabling institutional environment that helps shape inclusive outcomes.

Inclusive institutions create the incentives and opportunities necessary to harness creativity and entrepreneurship in society, whether in economic, social or political activity. They facilitate access to decision-making; promote transparency, openness and engagement; avoid policy capture; and contribute to aligning policies with the needs of society, including those of underserved or excluded social groups. In so doing, inclusive institutions allow for better decisions that are closer to society's needs, setting a foundation for successful policymaking and implementation. Indeed, Goal 16 of the Sustainable Development Goals calls for "effective, accountable and transparent institutions at all levels" and "responsive, inclusive, participatory and representative decision-making".

Achieving inclusive growth requires a holistic approach: Inclusive growth needs inclusive institutions and an investment in inclusive problem identification and decision making.

In the context of inclusive growth, inclusive institutions and inclusive policy making are essential to shape and inform policy goals and overall direction, guiding government action towards those outcomes that matter most for societal well-being.

Inclusive institutions can boost the impact of the public governance tools and processes along the policy cycle discussed in Chapter 2. Investing in inclusive problem identification and decision-making can enable a steering vision for inclusive growth at the macro level and more effective, tailored policies at the micro level. Innovative government-citizen partnerships can lead to better, cost-effective service delivery and increased access. Stakeholder engagement can be leveraged to inform programme implementation and evaluation. Mechanisms to curb undue influence can ensure transparency and integrity in decision-making, and thus, better outcomes. Diversity in the public sector workforce can boost performance and engagement and send a strong signal of inclusion (Figure 3.1).

Figure 3.1. Inclusive Institutions help shape inclusive growth outcomes

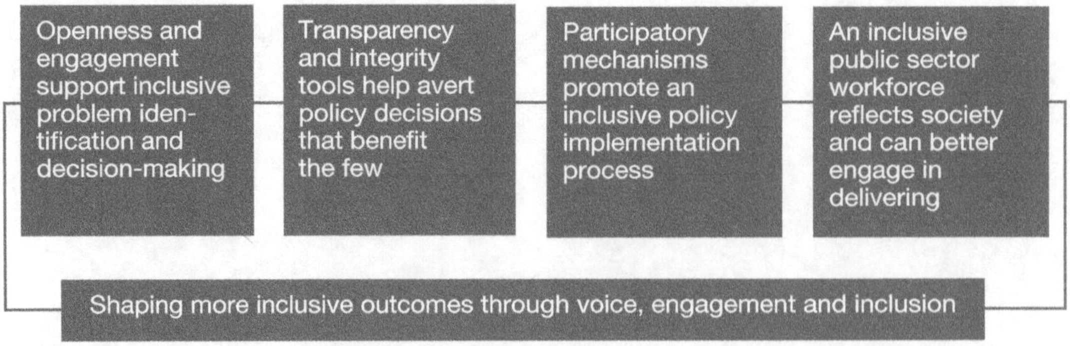

Openness and engagement support inclusive problem identification and decision-making	Transparency and integrity tools help avert policy decisions that benefit the few	Participatory mechanisms promote an inclusive policy implementation process	An inclusive public sector workforce reflects society and can better engage in delivering

Shaping more inclusive outcomes through voice, engagement and inclusion

However, despite wide recognition that inclusive institutions can contribute to inclusive growth, establishing the conditions for lasting changes is not without challenges.

Challenges are varied and may relate to inadequate representation of stakeholders, inaccessibility of information, obstacles to civic participation, inadequate use of inputs received or overall institutional attitudes, which may still be anchored in a top down approach to policy making. There is also a need to dispel the myths around stakeholder engagement more specifically. Even with the best intentions and the framework conditions in place, stakeholder engagement may fail to achieve an inclusive process and may even entail capture if not properly handled. Ultimately, there is a lack of systematic evaluation, hence a lack of evidence on the performance of inclusive institutions to support inclusive growth. More evidence on the impacts of stakeholder engagement, including context specific dimensions, and practical guidance on successful practices are much needed.

Building inclusive institutions is challenging: *While the contribution of inclusive institutions towards creating inclusive growth is widely recognised, we must continue to ensure adequate representation, provide usable information and gather evidence.*

Engaging stakeholders and preventing capture: Inclusive policy making through stakeholder engagement

Openness and stakeholder engagement can be leveraged to render the policy-making process more inclusive and informed, leading to policies that are fairer and closer to citizen's needs.

The OECD Guiding Principles for Open and Inclusive Policy Making emphasise that inclusion means not only that all citizens should have equal opportunities and multiple channels to access information, but also that they should be consulted (Box 3.2),[1] Consultation and engagement can help policy makers gather the necessary inputs and evidence to deal with the multidimensional nature of inclusive growth objectives and to identify policy trade-offs.

Box 3.2. Stakeholder engagement as a new paradigm of policy making

The notion of participation has evolved over recent years towards the concept of engagement. OECD (2015a) argues that participation typically refers to the involvement of individuals and groups in designing, implementing and evaluating a project or plan. Engagement goes beyond procedures and methods to consult and inform. As a result, concepts, such as co-creation and co-production, have emerged to describe the systematic pursuit of continuous co-operation between government agencies and stakeholders. Today, engagement with broader constituencies is identified as an important factor in determining whether institutions will be effective and enduring, in particular from informational and problem-solving perspectives.[2]

The concept of inclusive policy making through stakeholder engagement largely overlaps with that of open government. Open government can be defined as "the transparency of government actions, the accessibility of government services and information and the responsiveness of government to new ideas, demands and needs" (OECD, 2005).

Box 3.2. Stakeholder engagement as a new paradigm of policy making *(continued)*

In particular, inclusion is one of the two dimensions of open government (OECD, 2009). As a result, openness and inclusion represent the two pillars to deliver better policy outcomes not only for, but with, citizens. Today, inclusive policy making through stakeholder engagement is set to enhance government accountability, broaden citizens' influence on decisions and build civic capacity.

Source: Based on Alemanno (2015); OECD (2015a).

Stakeholder engagement creates a virtuous circle in which citizens become more deeply involved in policy choices, reforms and outcomes. But, if not handled properly, the engagement process can fail to ensure inclusive results and contribute to policy capture.

Through engagement, stakeholders develop a sense of ownership over policy choices, reforms and projects' outcomes.

This contributes to greater acceptance and legitimacy and, in turn, is likely to lead to better compliance with policies and regulations (Allan, 2014). At the same time, engagement enables external control of the decision-making process and strengthens accountability of the government as a whole and also of individual civil servants. For example, in the United States, the Rebuild by Design initiative created after the 2012 Hurricane Sandy brought together researchers, designers and Sandy-affected areas' businesses, policy makers and local groups to redevelop communities and better prepare for future storms. Three years after they started, local coalitions and community groups involved had taken ownership of the projects and worked to ensure the government implements them effectively.

In addition, stakeholder engagement can bring voice to those that have are most vulnerable to economic uncertainty and social exclusion (e.g. elderly, youth, unemployed, deprived or unserved segments of the population).

In Finland, a pilot service has been developed to combat the passive attitude of certain unprivileged segments of the population by providing health care (blood pressure and diabetes checks) in a familiar environment. The programme is aimed at hard-to-reach patients, who often have increased health risks and do not seek medical advice before clearly visible symptoms arise; it provides them with the knowledge and means for following their own health condition on a daily basis. In Ireland, a whole-of-government strategy on children and young people's participation in decision-making was launched in 2015 following extensive consultation (including 66 700 children and young people) (Box 20).

Preventing capture to safeguard inclusive growth

Averting policy capture is a crucial element to achieve and sustain inclusive growth.

Policy capture occurs when the interests of a narrow group dominate those of other stakeholders to the benefit of that narrow group (Box 3.3). In a democratic context, this involves the exclusion of parties and opinions and violates basic democratic norms

(Warren, 2003). When policy making is captured by a handful of powerful interests, rules may be bent to favour only the few in the society. The consequences include the erosion of democratic governance, the pulling apart of social cohesion, and the limiting of equal opportunities for all.

Policy capture exacts a high price. The consequences of policy capture include the erosion of democratic governance and the reduction of equal opportunity.

Box 3.3. Defining state, regulatory and policy capture

While state, regulatory and policy capture share common traits, they overlap only partially. In the case of state capture, it is the central government which is captured at a large scale, including parliamentary law-making (Fries, Lysenko and Polanec, 2003; Hellman, Jones and Kaufmann, 2003; McLean and McMillan, 2009); whereas in the case of regulatory capture, it is commonly a regulator, regulatory agency of an industry or the regulatory process in the industry which is captured (Etzioni, 2009). For example, capture occurs in regulatory agencies when private actors, seeking to reduce the cost of compliance, persuade regulators to alter rules or be lenient in enforcing those rules (Thomas et al., 2010).

Rather than looking at the function being captured, the analysis of policy capture encompasses any undue influence on policy making, hence taking into account the variety of captors and captor groups, as well as their practices to establish and maintain influence on policy making. A major difference to regulatory capture, on the one hand, is that capturing a regulatory agency responsible for implementing legislation remains vulnerable to external intervention, such as legislative change enacted by the parliament or put forward by the central government. Capturing a policy area, however, fends off any such uncertainty by controlling the policy process in a particular field either entirely or at any step of the policy-making process. On the other hand, capturing the central government and controlling most of its activities by any captor (group) is relatively rare in functioning democracies with an institutionalised separation of powers and regular turnover of governments.

Special interest groups or individuals attempt to influence policy makers in favour of a particular interest or issue. At the centre of policy capture networks stand exchanges of favours between private and public actors, which can be set up for one exchange or established and maintained on a regular, even highly institutionalised basis. In the latter case, policy capture is best characterised as a stable flow of mutual favours among the captor network. In this context, policy capture constitutes the collusion between high-level public actors – i.e. politicians or bureaucrats – and high-level private actors – i.e. businesspeople – to form a captor relationship. They can act as individuals or as part of a group (e.g. members of special interest groups or advisory groups). Furthermore, businesspeople and brokers can also act as professional lobbyists and public officials as well as private actors can be major players in the media landscape.

Source: OECD (forthcoming 2016). Safeguarding Inclusive Public Decision-Making by CPolicy Making in the Public Interest: Curbing the Risks of Policy Capture.

While high-spending areas, such as infrastructure and urban planning, are particularly vulnerable to the risk of capture, any policy-making process can be a target of powerful narrow interests.

Policy capture involves varieties of actors and means, but it usually takes place through unregulated lobbying, conflict of interests of public officials and unbalanced political finance (OECD, forthcoming). Lobbying is often perceived as an opaque activity of dubious integrity, which may result in undue influence, unfair competition and policy capture to the detriment of fair, impartial and effective policy making. Similarly, forms of conflict between private interests of public officials and their public duties may arise in the interaction between the public and private sectors, heightening the risks of policy capture. Moreover, political donations are a necessary component of the democratic process, enabling representation and facilitating democratic competition, but they need to be regulated appropriately to avoid undue influence and capture by interest groups (OECD, 2013a).

Policy capture can be ad hoc or institutionalised. It occurs when special interest groups or individuals attempt to influence policy makers in favour of a particular interest or issue. This can happen on an ad hoc basis, or be established and maintained on a regular, even highly institutionalised basis.

Remedies to secure unbiased and inclusive policy making include increasing transparency and integrity in lobbying and better managing conflict of interest.

Measures can be taken to regulate lobbying, recognising its importance for informed decision-making but curbing the risk of undue influence and unfair competition. With the adoption of the OECD Recommendation on Transparency and Integrity in Lobbying in 2010, countries are encouraged to introduce regulations to increase transparency in the interaction between the public officials and lobbyists, thus reducing policy capture. Improving the transparency and integrity of the policy-making process, particularly by using regulation to address concerns over lobbying, has been high on many governments' agendas including lobbying registry, code of conduct and pre/post public employment regulation.

How can you fight against policy capture? Measures can be taken which allow lobbying to fulfil its role in transmitting vital information while curbing the risk of undue influence.

Similarly, the OECD Guidelines for Managing Conflict of Interest in the Public Service provide policy makers with a set of tangible policy options based on promoting individual responsibility, supporting scrutiny and creating an appropriate organisational culture.

Institutional measures, such as external audit and verification, or other internal supervisory approaches are widely observed, while asset and private interest disclosure by public officials continues to be an essential tool for managing conflict of interest. Ensuring that the integrity of policy making is not compromised by public officials' private interest is a crucial anti-corruption measure, although it remains challenging in many countries. Modernising the management of asset declarations by public officials will facilitate increasing transparency and accountability to the public. Finally, options are available for regulating political finance on a context specific basis, including by promoting the use of online technologies for greater transparency and scrutiny, allocating sufficient human and financial resources to the electoral monitoring bodies and mapping potential integrity and compliance risks.

Shaping vision and delivery through stakeholder engagement

Stakeholder engagement in shaping policies

Engagement of stakeholders is increasingly allowing countries to define national priorities as delineated in policies, laws and regulations.

Countries have made progress in involving stakeholders both in the process of setting national priorities (Box 3.4) and in developing new laws and regulations. As an example recent evidence shows that a majority of OECD countries have implemented a requirement to engage stakeholders in developing both primary and secondary regulations (OECD, 2015b). The requirement for stakeholder engagement is implemented through various government instruments, including in a number of cases through constitutional requirements.

Stakeholders have new roles in shaping policy: Recent evidence shows that a majority of OECD countries have implemented requirements to engage stakeholders in developing both primary and secondary regulations, although often late in the process.

The importance of stakeholder engagement in reviewing existing legislative frameworks is also widely understood among OECD countries.

The majority of countries report mechanisms for stakeholder engagement in ex post evaluations of regulation (OECD, 2015b). The Red Tape Challenge initiative in the United Kingdom for instance relies on using external input from a wide spectrum of stakeholders to simplify existing regulations. The Danish Burden Hunters project and the Swedish Better Regulation Hunt are examples of targeted, proactive approaches of using close co-operation with stakeholders to analyse existing regulatory burdens and to find ways to simplify existing regulations.

Box 3.4. Examples of national policies shaped by stakeholder engagement

The government of Lithuania, for instance, has engaged in an in-depth process to define its national strategy "Lithuania 2030". The State Progress Council, led by the centre of government, was responsible for the drafting process of the strategy; government authorities, business leaders, community groups and prominent public figures participated in its development. Three working groups were set up on smart economy, smart governance and smart society. The consultation involved the national level and Lithuanians living abroad. The Council also travelled to meet with mayors, municipality representatives, young people and non-governmental organisations. Innovative approaches were developed to involve harder-to-reach groups, including the youth and the elderly. The outcome is a national strategy which is guiding the policies of the whole country and whose implementation is monitored in an inclusive process (OECD, 2015c).

The Northern Ireland Health Strategy "Investing for Health" (2002) was the outcome of a comprehensive stakeholder engagement process and a partnership among different departments, public bodies and district councils. The engagement process included consultations, a debate in the Assembly, involvement of the Community Development and Health Network, and innovative approaches such as an arts project and a photo competition. The resulting strategy took a broader approach to health than originally planned, focusing on improving well-being and reducing health inequalities (DHSSPS, 2002).

Stakeholder engagement is shaping better policies. "Lithuania 2030" and "Investing for Health" in Northern Ireland are two examples of programmes in which stakeholders have helped to shape the policy process.

However, establishing the legal basis for stakeholder engagement is insufficient to ensure its effective implementation.

A typical engagement on regulatory proposals still takes place at the final stage of the process through a public consultation over the Internet or consultation with selected groups such as business associations and trade unions. This is generally too late to influence the process and may show a largely procedural use of the tools of stakeholder engagement (OECD, 2015b) (Figure 3.2).

Figure 3.2. When do consultations happen on primary and subordinate regulations? (2014)

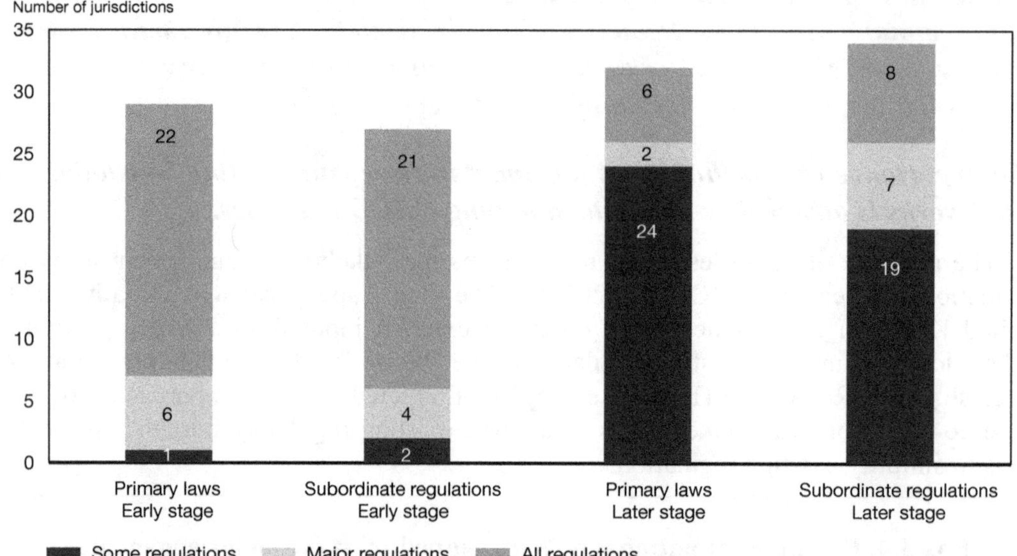

Notes: Early stage refers to stakeholder engagement that occurs at the outset to inform officials about the nature of the problem and to feed discussions on possible solutions. Later stage refers to stakeholder engagement where the preferred solution has been identified and/or a draft version of the regulation has been issued. Based on data from 34 countries and the European Commission as of December 2014.

Source: OECD (2015b).

A shift towards accessibility and engagement in budgeting can play an important role in pursuing inclusive growth objectives.

Traditionally, budget processes have tended to be relatively opaque and technical, and mainly the institutions of government and policy 'insiders' have controlled and understood them. To address this challenge, the OECD Best Practices on Budget Transparency promotes opening up budgetary processes and documentation to facilitate a more informed debate on budgetary choices. In recent years, however, the concept of budget transparency has evolved to include issues of policy responsiveness, citizen engagement and broader societal participation in the policy-making process. This is illustrated in the "OECD Recommendation of the Council on Budgetary Governance"

(2015d), which calls for ensuring that budget documents and data are open, transparent and accessible, as well as providing for an inclusive, participative and realistic debate on budgetary choices. However, while much progress has been made across OECD countries in increasing the transparency of budget documents and processes, less progress has been made in going beyond transparency to active civic engagement.

Inclusive growth and budgeting: Transparency and access to information removes some of the opacity and complexity of the budgetary process and allows the inclusion of non-specialist stakeholders in the policy cycle.

Stakeholder engagement is increasingly conducted at subnational and local levels. Regions and localities operate at a more manageable scale for many forms of stakeholder engagement.

They provide useful vehicles for translating national policy design and implementation at the local level, increasing national policy effectiveness. Also, regions and localities are responsible for much of the service delivery and public investment that determines economic growth and people's well-being.[3] Indeed, many policy experiments, such as smart cities, participative budgeting or co-production of social service delivery, are carried out at the city or regional levels. For example, many regions have established regional councils that combine elected officials, businesses, social partners and other relevant stakeholders; these include universities, which contribute to promoting regional development strategies and oversee implementation, such as Denmark's Regional Growth Forums (OECD, 2012). Others, like the city of Paris, have allowed its citizens to decide on investment priorities (Box 3.5).

Stakeholders are essential in shaping subnational government policy. Regions and localities are responsible for much of the service delivery and public investment that determines economic growth and well-being. Stakeholder consultation is increasingly part of the policy process.

Box 3.5. Participative budgeting in Paris

Through the so-called "budget participatif", citizens can vote among several proposed projects and are asked to select the investments that they consider most valuable in a context where a limited budget does not permit implementing all proposals.

Since 2014 the municipality of Paris gives its citizens the opportunity to decide on the use of 5% of its investment budget, which amounts to 0.5 billion EUR in 2014-20. The aim is to involve citizens in municipal politics to foster social cohesion and to learn their preferences. It builds on the principles of open government and promotes a stronger relation between citizens, their representatives and the public institutions.

In the 2015 edition of the budget participatif, participation was deepened by providing citizens with the opportunity to propose projects that would then be voted on (Mairie de Paris, 2015). The project tries to harness creative ideas of Parisians, and the process is as follows: (i) Parisians propose their ideas for investment projects on a website; (ii) The municipality evaluates the feasibility of the proposals; and (iii) project proposals are submitted to vote by Parisians.

Source: Mairie de Paris (2015).

Stakeholder engagement is also reshaping service delivery

Stakeholder engagement is increasingly seen as a response to the challenges of fostering quality service delivery.

There is growing recognition that services work better when designed and delivered in partnership with citizens, and that listening to stakeholders' insights can foster innovation in service delivery practices and better risk management. In the water sector, for instance, many utilities rely on governance boards where stakeholders have a say in strategic orientations, or advisory boards in which different categories of actors take collective decisions. As an example, the public water utility in Grenoble, France, has engaged with consumer associations regarding setting water tariffs for the last 20 years (OECD, 2015e). By the same token, safety and health care are often co-produced, as a desired level of outcomes implies directly involving individuals, for example in monitoring their own health conditions and changing eating habits. Innovation units and laboratories have been active in fostering co-production approaches in public services (Box 3.6).

Listening to stakeholders' insights can foster innovation in service delivery, better risk management and greater quality in service delivery.

Box 3.6. Finland's living lab environments

Living Lab is a new, innovative structure that combines different stakeholders in order to test and develop user-driven products for elderly people and elderly care. It results from the co-operation between the social and health services of the City of Pori, Finland, based on their need to find more efficient models for elderly care. The purpose was to test and develop technological solutions in order to provide a better quality of life and more dignity for elderly people as well as to improve safety, prevent loneliness and support for elderly people living at home.

The Living Lab provides an environment where citizens (elderly people, relatives) participate actively in the development and usability testing of welfare technologies along with service professionals and welfare technology companies. Testing also took place in real life contexts, i.e. in elderly people's homes. The Living Lab Model has provided information of the latest technology solutions for public health care to support procurement, has improved nursing processes and the technological skills of elderly care personnel, has increased co-operation between elderly people, relatives and nursing personnel and has supported home care. It has also improved business opportunities and facilitated co-operation between municipalities, business and other stakeholders.

Source: OPSI Database.

Leveraging tools for engagement, from information to co-creation

Modalities of stakeholder engagement

Governments can choose from a continuum of engagement mechanisms.

Modalities vary from basic communication of information, which is the weakest form of engagement, to full co-production, co-delivery and co-evaluation, which involves a balanced share of powers among the stakeholders. Each of these modalities of engagement has different objectives and impacts and requires specific tools for their implementation (Figure 3.3).

There are a number of tools to help engage stakeholders, each with a specific function and involving citizens to different degrees in the policy-making process.

Figure 3.3. Levels of stakeholder engagement

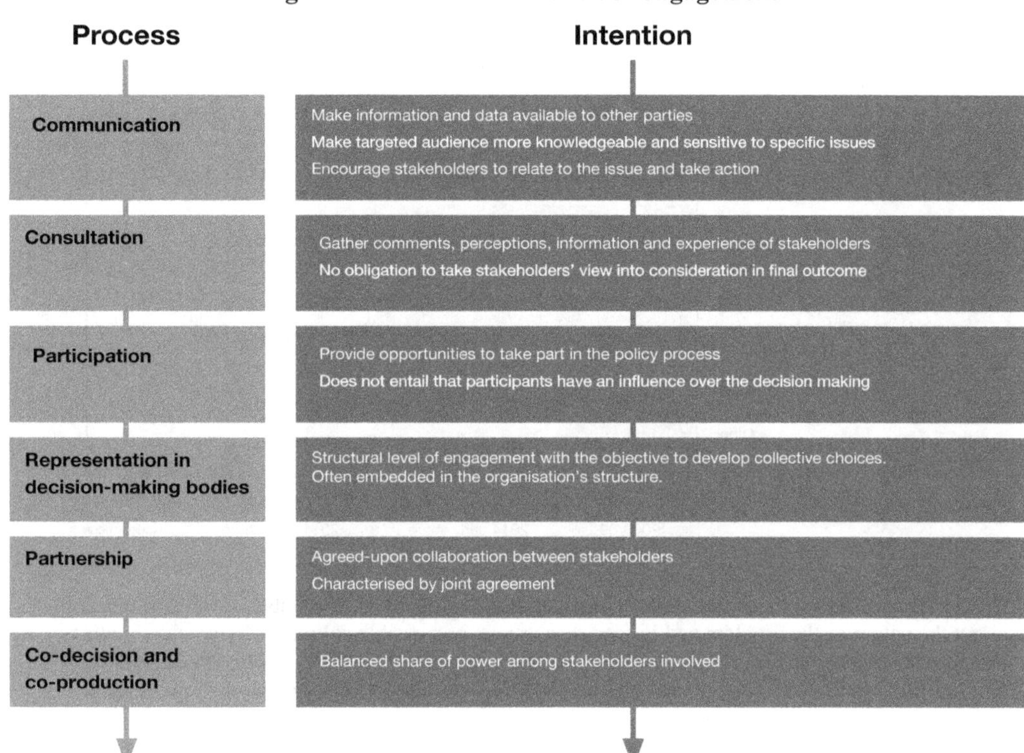

As illustrated in different policy areas and sectors, there is a variety of tools and mechanisms for engagement.

These are sector and policy area specific and may illustrate various depths of engagement. For example, in the case of regulatory policy, evidence shows that some tools are used more frequently in the early stages of stakeholder engagement (e.g. informal consultation with selected groups), while other tools are used later in the engagement process, such as posting draft regulations on the Internet or formal consultations with social partners (Box 3.7) and all interested stakeholders (Figure 3.4). Arms-length institutions including transparency councils, anti-corruption agencies, or ombudsman offices provide an opportunity for ex post engagement, as citizens can lodge a complaint against the public administration. Over time, engagement has evolved from sharing information with a reduced set of participants, such as advisory groups, towards greater inclusion, particularly through web-based consultations. There has also been an evolution from unilateral information provision towards active encouragement of stakeholder participation.

While the use of some types of regulatory consultation has diminished since 2008, new technologies enabling two-way consultation are on the rise.

Figure 3.4. Types of consultation in regulatory policy (December 2014)

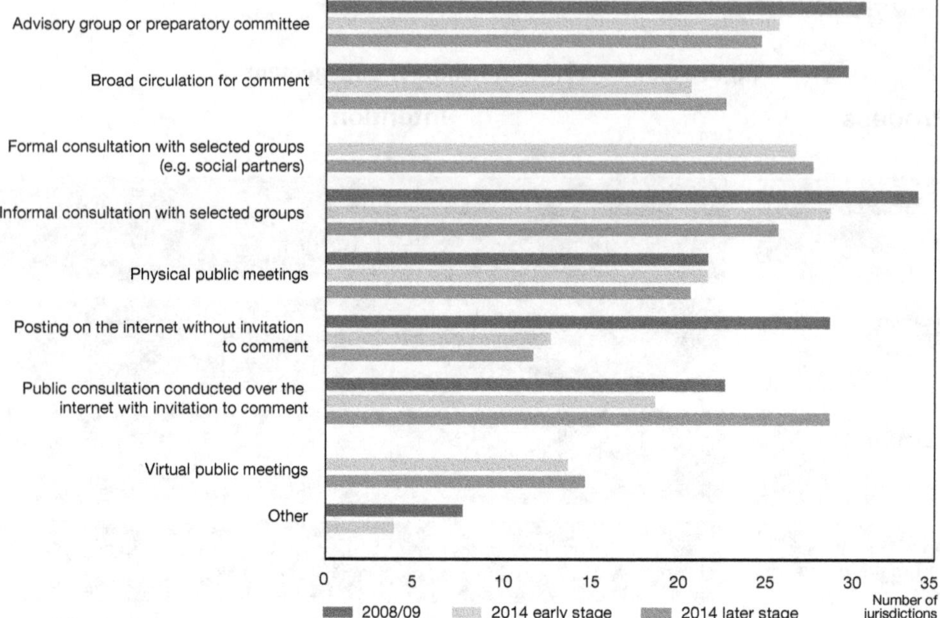

Notes: Early stage refers to stakeholder engagement that occurs at the outset to inform officials about the nature of the problem and to feed discussions on possible solutions. Later stage refers to stakeholder engagement where the preferred solution has been identified and/or a draft version of the regulation has been issued. Based on data from 34 countries and the European Commission.

Source: OECD (2015b).

Box 3.7. Examples of formal regulatory consultation with social partners

Formal consultations (defined by exchanges with selected interested parties where the proceedings are formally recorded) are frequently or always conducted in 14 OECD countries. Consultation with social partners is common in the rule-making process of the European Union (EU). The EU recognises and promotes the role of the social partners at its level, taking into account the diversity of national systems (Article 152 of the EU Treaty). It is a statutory requirement for all EU-level social and employment regulation (Articles 154 and 155 of the EU Treaty). This "EU social dialogue" process is organised in two steps: at the early stage of the process the European Commission consults the social partners on the broad features of a future regulatory initiative; then, the Commission consults the partners on a specific proposal. If, after each of these steps, the social partners fail to reach a common position and engage bipartite negotiations, the Commission can proceed unilaterally with its own proposal.

In Germany, consultation with social partners is formally required by law. According to the 2011 Joint Rules of Procedure, ministries must consult early and extensively with "associations". This refers to unions of natural or legal persons or groups to promote common interests including employers' associations and associations of workers and employees. According to the findings of the EU-15 Better Regulation project, those in the system apparently like this traditional method of consultation and feel that their economic and societal interests are heard and taken into consideration.

Box 3.7. Examples of formal regulatory consultation with social partners *(continued)*

Belgium enjoys a long-standing tradition (some 120 years) of consulting social partners on all economic and social regulations. Consultation in this case aims to provide comments before a regulation is adopted, to plan its entering into force, and/or to give advice on implementing and monitoring regulations. This usually takes place through various working groups and permanent committees (such as the National Council of Labour, Economy Central Council and Competition Council). They are considered as "social parliaments". In addition, each federated entity has established its own social and economic council, bringing together social partners.

In South Africa, the creation of the National Economic Development and Labour Council (NEDLAC) in the post-Apartheid era was an important step in ensuring inclusive policy and law-making processes. The NEDLAC includes representation of South African trade unions and employer federations.

Source: OECD (2015b).

Formal consultation of social partners is a statutory requirement for all EU-level social and employment regulation.

Modalities for stakeholder engagement also vary in nature.

The OECD Survey on Stakeholder Engagement in the Water Sector identified 24 mechanisms that can be categorised into two types: formal mechanisms that have institutional and legal ground, and informal mechanisms that are not institutionalised but can be implemented for a large variety of issues and at the discretion of the convener of the engagement process (OECD, 2015e). These different mechanisms have their strengths and weaknesses (Figure 3.5). Moreover, engagement modalities vary in terms of the amount of time they take, the number of stakeholders they involve and the amount of resources they require. Similarly, different tools may apply best to different steps of the policy cycle (i.e. design, implementation or evaluation) or to different categories of actors.

Stakeholder engagement mechanisms can be formal, with institutional and legal grounds, and informal. The latter are not institutionalised and can be employed at the discretion of the convener of the engagement process.

Figure 3.5. Strengths and weaknesses of engagement mechanisms: Examples from the water sector

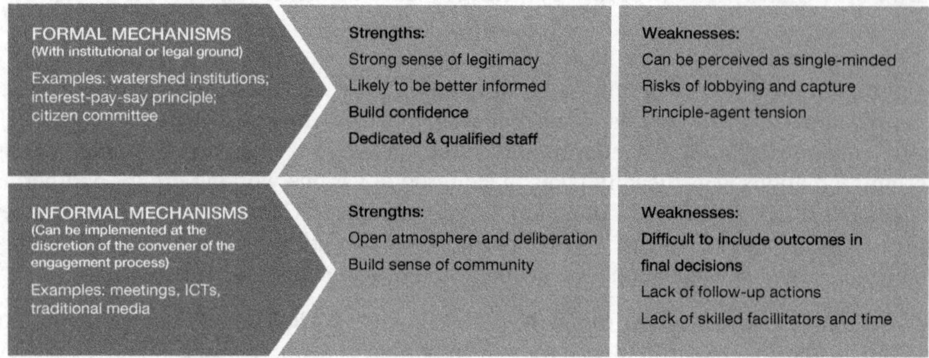

Source: OECD (2015h).

Knowing the stakeholders

Stakeholder engagement requires thorough identification of the relevant stakeholders.

Knowing who is responsible for what and at which level is an essential starting point to identify conflicts, grey areas and trade-offs to be managed. Stakeholder mapping can shed light on the core and influential players and bring attention to the interactions with, and the impacts of, stakeholders in other areas that influence a given sector or policy area. Important aspects need to be taken into account in mapping stakeholders, including identifying the relevant players (primary decision-maker, influential actors in the area, actors with power to obstruct decisions, etc.); the potential of stakeholders to contribute to, or hinder, decision-making and implementation processes; and the interest of the identified players in the issue at hand. Critical for inclusive growth, such mapping has the potential to identify the categories of stakeholders that are often excluded.

Access to information: The basis of stakeholder engagement

The right to access information is a fundamental pillar of inclusive policy making and stakeholder engagement.

Today, most OECD countries have stand-alone freedom of information legislation, or the right to access information is embedded within other laws or regulations. However, OECD governments are struggling to fully institutionalise openness and inclusiveness through access to information. In part, this is due to regulatory and implementation challenges related to their scope (e.g. entities subject to the law), and to the extent and nature of information disclosed (e.g. exceptions). Effectively and transparently implementing the legal framework is essential to safeguard the principles and objectives of the legislation (OECD, 2013a). One of way of doing so is through effective, accessible channels for stakeholders to seek redress in their interaction with the public administration through for example information commissioners or ombudsman offices.

Many OECD governments are striving to fully institutionalise openness and inclusiveness through access to information. But information is only one component of the engagement process.

Still, the availability of information is an insufficient step.

It is the attributes of the information disclosed, including its relevance in relation to the concerns of stakeholders, and its usability that make the difference regarding the actual use of information to influence policy decisions (OECD, 2013a). Simply providing information does not by itself give users the opportunity to exercise accountability or participate in public processes. First, data is often disseminated in a way that makes it difficult for average citizens and even civil society or the media to understand, for example if it is presented as aggregated reports or in highly technical language. Second, stakeholders must have the capacity, and the necessary incentives, to use the information (Baena and Vieyra, 2011).

The role of new technologies: Open government data (OGD) and social media

The steady integration of new technologies, including cloud computing, social media and mobile technology, is giving rise to new forms of public engagement.

Digitally enabled participation and production of services is changing people's expectations about their relationships with governments. As a result, the OECD Recommendation on Digital Government Strategies highlights the need for new public governance approaches to support a shift from governments' anticipating citizens' and businesses' needs (citizen-centric approaches) to citizens and businesses determining their own needs and addressing them in partnership with governments (citizen-driven approaches).

Indeed, leveraging Open Government Data (OGD) for more inclusive policy making implies adopting community-oriented approaches to engage non-government actors, such as civil society, academia and businesses.

This requires a move from individual steps to implement OGD to a more concerted government approach to engaging with existing and potential data producers and re-users. Communities, networks and events of different types can help the government achieve greater reach, take-up and eventually impact for OGD. This can include setting up more regular and intensive modes of engagement, including user groups, meet-ups, contests and partnerships (OECD, 2015f). Country experiences offer interesting insights in this regard (Box 3.8).

Citizens and businesses know their own needs. Open Government Data is an important tool in allowing a citizen- and business-driven approach to designing services that better meet those needs.

Box 3.8. Community-based approaches to Open Government Data in OECD countries

The United Kingdom has championed a user-oriented approach to open data release in a range of ways, including: establishing a public inventory of government data; creating an online data-request process (through data.gov.uk) so that citizens can directly apply for datasets; establishing an Open Data User Group (made up of government representatives, civil society, academia and business stakeholders) to advise government on public sector data that should be prioritised for release as open data, and the Release of Data Fund to remove barriers to releasing public data, support projects that build capacity among data owners, and build new platforms and services with open data. The government is now exploring ways to further embed these mechanisms into its approach to open data release.

In France, the Prime Minister's Open Government Data unit Etalab holds monthly lunch-time events (Bonjour Data) that are free for any interested parties to attend and discuss ideas and issues around OGD (www.etalab.gouv.fr/event/bonjour-data/all). In parallel to this unstructured, open-for-all set of meetings, the French government has been actively engaging government and non-government actors through its DataConnexions network.

The German government held a public consultation in 2015 about the directions to take on Open Government Data (www.open-data-aktionsplan.de/). Germany has had a beta version of its open data portal in place for some time (www.govdata.de/). The public online consultation represents an intensified commitment to OGD and allows the public to influence the national government's open data action plan for the near future. It is important to underline that this online consultation is only one step of a larger process that will now lead to workshops, drafting of an action plan and eventually resubmission of the draft action plan for public consultation before it becomes the German federal government's official action plan.

In Spain, a number of collaboration channels have been established among actors of the open data community the Public Private Partnership Forum on the Re-use of Public Sector Information, an open web community for partnerships between different stakeholders, and a virtual community of public administrations. These communities address issues that might hamper the publication of information (technological, regulatory and standardisation of information) and share good practices. Moreover, they collaborate in the activities related to open data, including the Catalogue of Public Information datos.gob.es, currently with 8 492 datasets; initiatives of promotion and support, training, and participation in national and international events; and the DCAT-based standard for interoperability. Spain received the Award for Innovation in Public Administration 2013 and the EU Prize LAPSI platform 2012.

Governments are mobilising around Open Government Data creating innovative and inclusive partnerships between government and non-government actors.

Social media have proven to be a powerful vehicle to help share opinions and the desire for action, which in turn attracts the attention of mainstream media and decision-makers.

Channelling disparate interests and rallying for action is not new in itself, but social media and the Internet more generally empower less organised and less established groups and give them relatively inexpensive means to rally ad hoc support around common causes. With these tools in hand, formerly dispersed individuals or less well-resourced groups obtain greater agenda-setting power, which is important for inclusive policy making. Although using social media still tends to be more widespread among better educated individuals (Figure 3.6), the Never Seconds blog in Scotland is a good example of how social media can empower people who had no previous effective recourse to existing intermediaries. Through the blog, a nine-year-old schoolgirl and her parents raised awareness on the low nutritional value of school meals, triggering policy responses.[4]

Social media can empower less-organised groups. Through social media, formerly isolated individuals or less well-resourced groups can obtain greater agenda-setting power, which is important for inclusive policy making.

Figure 3.6. Use of social media in OECD countries

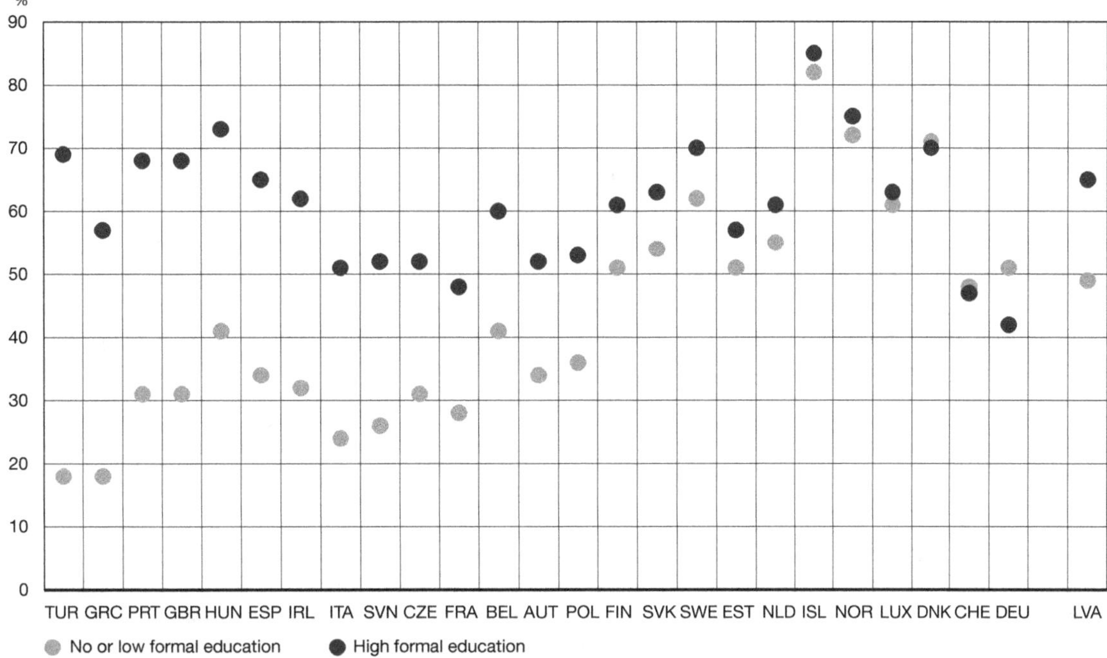

Source: OECD (2015g).

Social media can also enable governments to be more responsive to demands from stakeholders.

They make it easier for governments to bypass or complement traditional means for gauging public sentiment, such as opinion polls and organised interest groups. Using social media for "active listening" can help governments de-escalate problems or satisfy demands before they become the issues of major discontent. Indeed, online petitions, for example, have become a powerful tool in many countries. The Latvian parliament accepted the online petition platform www.manabalss.lv in 2011 as a valid means for the public to propose new legislation. The parliament accepted a new rule of procedure whereby a threshold of 10 000 valid citizen signatures (equivalent to around 0.5% of the population) would require the government to put a legal proposal onto the parliament's legislative agenda. So far, 12 out of over 650 proposals have been discussed in parliament. Some have become legislation, including the right of judicial authorities to access information on civil servants' offshore accounts.

Social media are also providing a powerful tool for co-production in public service by providing real-time opportunities for participation and feedback.

Some of the opportunities to transform public service delivery that are often cited are: providing new – possibly more efficient – channels to deliver public information, goods and services; identifying new means and resources for collaboration in the creation and delivery of public goods and services; opening up new ways to understand and anticipate user needs at various stages in the service design and delivery process; and re-designing services in more iterative ways. One example that combines several of those aspects is the continued social media engagement of the Spanish national police, which has from the beginning aimed at being as inclusive as possible, resulting in greater trust by society and mission-critical results for the institution (Box 3.9).

Social media can provide real-time participation and feedback, offering new possibilities for collaboration in the creation and delivery of public goods and services while opening up new ways to anticipate user needs.

Box 3.9. Spanish National Police: Inclusive use of social media

Policing heavily depends on people's confidence and co-operation to deliver an effective public service. The Spanish national police force (Cuerpo Nacional de Policía de España) early on identified the potential of social media. It started using social media in 2010 as an additional lever to engage the population and improve its services. The commitment was backed up with financial and human resources and the recruitment of a social media expert.

Today, a dedicated team is available to interact on various social media platforms to inform people and to prevent, dissuade and combat crime. Its Twitter account has over 1.5 million followers (@Policia), its Facebook page has over 250 000 fans (Policía Nacional) and the videos on its YouTube have been viewed 6 million times (Policía).

A large part of this social media success is due to a deliberate choice of topics and style. Unlike many other government institutions, the Spanish police do not use social media for corporate communications such as relaying the agendas of its leadership or to issue traditional press releases. It rather uses social networks to support the police's primary mission by sending content-rich messages that are earnest, use plain language and are often humorous or provocative in order to attract attention in the busy environment that social networks are today.

Source: Mickoleit (2014), Fernández Guerra (2014).

Addressing the challenge of engagement

Strengthening administrative capacity, participation literacy and reach

Effective stakeholder engagement is not without challenges.

These challenges include: (i) low administrative capacity, weak mandates, planning or incentives, or a non-supportive administrative culture; (ii) difficulties in accessing hard-to-reach social groups, in particular under-represented segments of the population (whether on the basis of social or economic backgrounds, ethnic-, cultural- or gender-based identity or location factors); and (iii) weak participation, including issues of literacy, accessibility or perceived impact of the time and effort required to engage.

Stakeholder engagement is essential but challenging. These challenges can include low administrative capacity, difficulty in accessing hard-to-reach social groups, including under-represented segments of the population, and weak participation due to literacy issues or perceptions of the commitment required by the engagement process.

Building an administrative culture to support stakeholder engagement requires reinforcing core public service values throughout the public administration.

This means clearly identifying the values – both those that drive stakeholder engagement in the public sector, such as openness, transparency, accessibility and equal opportunity, as well as those such as impartiality, independence, objectivity and honesty, which require civil servants to value balanced and sober evidence-based policy advice and to "speak truth to power". These values need to be trained, communicated, discussed, and reinforced including through their inclusion in codes of conduct and competency frameworks, and their use in the hiring and evaluation decisions. Many OECD counties provide ad hoc training for public officials, including guidelines and lessons learned to help implement a cultural change (OECD, 2014a).

Governments must also go beyond traditional consultation processes to target the "willing but unable" and the "able but unwilling" in order to support inclusive growth objectives.

Despite being affected by policy, some social groups are unlikely to engage effectively when given the opportunity to do so, because of a combination of lack of awareness, low participation literacy and information overload. This is unfortunate, because these groups contribute with "situated knowledge" (Farina and Newart). By contrast, well-organised interest groups are more effective in using the traditional channels of communication with government.

At the same time, governments must strive to increase the appeal of participation for people who are able but unwilling to participate due to subjective barriers, such as a low interest in politics or a lack of trust in the meaningful use of input into the consultation process (OECD, 2009). Civil society networks or umbrella organisations can be government partners and take on the role of reaching out to wider society. Various examples exist, such as Involve in the United Kingdom, which co-ordinates government's consultation on open government.

For a variety of reasons, certain social groups are unable or unwilling to participate in the stakeholder engagement process. Other groups are highly organised and highly vocal. Governments must overcome this 'participation conundrum' and strive to hear the voices of all people affected by policy.

Specific techniques and tools may be needed for encouraging underrepresented groups to participate.

The forthcoming OECD Recommendation on Gender Equality in Public Life, for example, calls for integrating gender analysis into citizen engagement initiatives. This is one tool to ensure fair representation of both women and men during public consultations.

Various examples of gender-sensitive good stakeholder engagement practices can be found in OECD member and partner countries (Box 3.10).

Box 3.10 Examples of gender-sensitive stakeholder engagement practices

Spain's Women Participation Council provides a channel for input by women's associations and groups into the policy-making process and matters related to gender equality.

Enlarging the involvement of stakeholders has also been prioritised in Latin American contexts, where there is a trend towards ensuring equitable representation from civil society, women's organisations, academics and other experts on gender equality councils or commissions.

Greece's National Programme for Gender Equality 2010-2013 was developed through extensive consultation with women's organisations. The programme itself made a commitment to "ongoing and systematic consultation with civil society on Programme implementation" using an interactive e-portal and reform of the National Committee for Equality between Men and Women that emphasises developing consultation and co-operating with civil society (OECD, 2014b).

In the Middle East and North Africa region, there are also examples of engaging women's non-governmental organisations in developing key laws (e.g. in Jordan, Lebanon, Morocco and the Palestinian Authority). Thus, in Jordan and the Palestinian Authority, civil society partners are consulted on legislation and regulations in sectors identified as key priority areas by the country's main gender institution (OECD, 2014b).

Young people and social media go together, yet governments have not been very successful in using the Internet to link up with and engage youth.

Engaging with youth is another case in point.

The voice of the youth is not always heard in policy debates, despite their high stakes in their outcomes and their potential input to find innovative solutions to shape a better future. Given that young people tend to be familiar with technology, it seems intuitive that governments could use social media to genuinely engage them. However, governments are not very successful in linking up with young people over the Internet: on average only 40% of young Europeans interact online with the public administration. In addition, although most young Europeans use social media (85% on average), only a minority are interested in using social media to engage in anything of a political or civic nature (Mickoleit, 2014).

To some extent, failure to engage youth may be due to stereotypical approaches to social media that focus on asserting government presence without due consideration for context. For example, in the United Kingdom a study found that around two-thirds of youth prefer to talk to someone in person rather than online and that one-quarter of unemployed young people are uncomfortable filling in job applications online (UK Prince's Trust, 2014). This is the kind of context data that decision-makers need to consider when designing social media strategies and guidelines that are supposed to address young people's concerns. Still, social media for youth participation holds promise. The prospect of engaging around one in five young people is already a success in countries like France, Iceland, Italy and Spain.

While including young people's voices in the policy process can require more effort in the short term, policies stand to gain in the long term.

For this reason, OECD countries are increasingly looking for ways to integrate youth voices into the policy and decision-making processes. This can include giving a voice through a national strategy or policy on children and young people's participation in decision-making, setting up local child and youth councils and a national youth parliament as in Ireland (Box 20) or engaging youth in the policy-making process. In Korea, youth participation organisations involved over 100 000 beneficiaries around 357 policy-making projects. In Italy, since 1997, the Chamber of Deputies has organised a Youth in the Law Hall process to introduce students to law development in the Piedmont region. Youth non-governmental organisations, acting as an intermediary, can also be supportive in raising young people's interest in participating in policy making.[5, 6]

OECD countries are increasingly looking for ways to integrate youth voices into the policy and decision-making process. What are the ways your country gives youth a voice?

Box 3.11 Examples from Ireland and the United Kingdom

In Ireland, the National Strategy on Children and Young People's Participation in Decision-making, 2015-2020, aims to have the voice of children and young people heard in decisions that affect their daily lives, including those that affect their education, health and well-being. Led by the Department of Children and Youth Affairs (DCYA), the strategy also promotes leadership and capacity building for professionals working with and on behalf of children and young people. The priority action in the strategy for DCYA is the establishment of a Children and Young People's Participation Hub, which will support Government departments and other organisations in implementing the strategy. The Comhairle na nÓg are Local Child and Youth Councils (www.comhairlenanog.ie) (ages 12-17) that give a voice to youth in the development of local policies and services in two ways: working on topics of importance to young people; and acting as a consultative forum for adult decision-makers in the locality. Every Comhairle na nÓg holds an Annual General Meeting to identify key topics and select its committee (attendance from 80-200 young people). The Dáil na nÓg is the National Youth Parliament for 12-18 year-olds and is a biennial event. Two hundred delegates from the 31 Comhairle na nÓg are elected as delegates to Dáil na nÓg. The DCYA funds and oversees Dáil na nÓg, which is hosted by the Minister for Children and Youth Affairs. Each of the 31 Comhairle na nÓg elects one representative to the Comhairle na nÓg National Executive to serve for a two-year period. The role of the National Executive is to follow up on the top recommendation from the previous Dáil na nÓg and seek to have it implemented, with support from the DCYA.

In the United Kingdom, the Cabinet Office promotes youth engagement and consultation at both national and local levels. The British Youth Council delivers a number of initiatives, such as the UK Youth Parliament (UKYP), Make Your Mark and the Youth Select Committee. UKYP is a youth organisation made up of 600 democratically elected members aged between 11 and 18 years. Members are elected to represent the views of young people in their area both to government and to national and local youth service providers. Make Your Mark is the largest ballot of youth views in the United Kingdom. It involves young people (aged 11-18) in debating and voting on issues that concern them. The priority topics are then debated in the annual sitting in the House of Commons. Finally, the Youth Select Committee brings together a group of 11 young people aged 15-18 to hold an annual inquiry into a key issue which young people care about. Their inquiry mirrors the process of a real parliamentary select committee.

Source: Based on information provided by the Department of Health and Children, Ireland, and by the Cabinet Office, United Kingdom.

Engaging stakeholders should never be a box-ticking exercise but must be followed up with feedback on comments received and on how they were used (or not) in the policy process.

While governments use a wider range of tools to reach out to users and citizens, a more proactive approach is needed to raise awareness and promote a culture of participation among stakeholders.

In order to reach a wider public, policy issues need to be framed in the language of the constituencies and be brought to where they are. For example, the budgeting process is traditionally viewed as a complex technocratic exercise with little scope for active input from citizens. Addressing this challenge requires a focus on promoting fiscal literacy, so that citizens and parliamentarians alike can better understand their potential role in a modern budget process, and in turn their potential impacts on advancing inclusive growth outcomes.

Effective engagement also calls on governments to provide adequate feedback on the comments received and on how they were (or were not) incorporated into policy proposals.

Indeed, some regulators in OECD countries are required to provide this kind of feedback (Figure 3.7), but this practice is not uniform across policy areas. Failure to offer feedback may lead to cynicism among stakeholders and decreased willingness to repeat such experience. At the same time, demonstrating to stakeholders that engagement[7] is inclusive and worthwhile helps prevent backlash and consultation fatigue. In France, for example, an evaluation of stakeholder engagement activities of the Alsace-Moselle inter-municipal public water service provider showed a steady increase in confidence in the service provider from elected officials (95% of satisfaction rate) and users (80%) (OECD, 2015e).

Figure 3.7 Obligation of regulators to provide feedback on comments (December 2014)

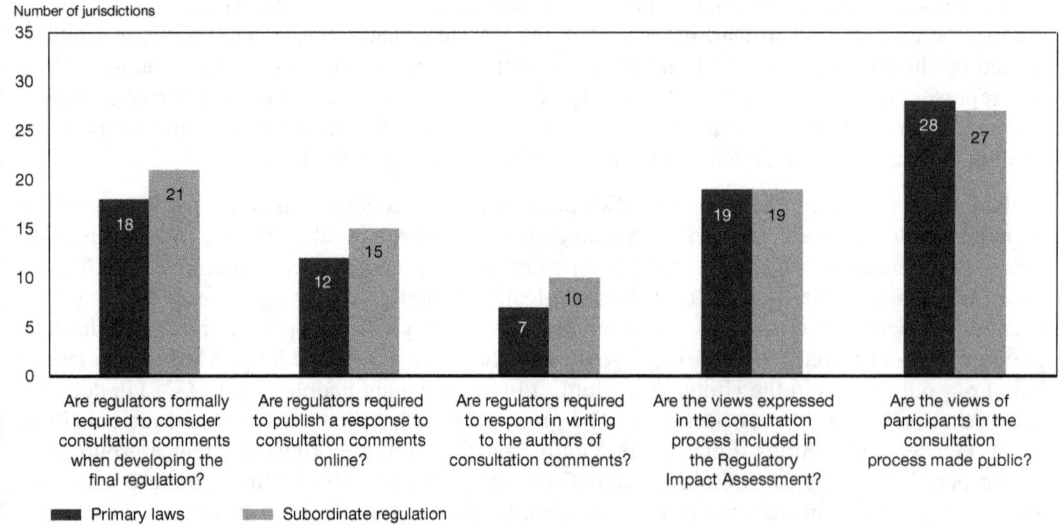

Note: Based on data from 34 countries and the European Commission.

Source: OECD (2015b).

When it comes to stakeholder engagement, engagement tools are important, but so is understanding their effectiveness. Better knowledge of what works and what does not is required.

The performance of stakeholder engagement to support inclusive policy making lacks systematic evaluation.

Much attention has been devoted to developing engagement tools, rather than on measuring their effectiveness. As a result, there is a significant evaluation gap in public engagement (OECD, 2001). This is true for both offline and online forms of engagement.[8] Anecdotal evidence shows that co-production can help tackle service failures, promote inclusiveness and participation, and reduce delivery costs. For instance, peer-to-peer support schemes have proved successful in schools to address achievement gaps and promote greater inclusiveness and participation; community-based approaches have also proved useful in developing more inclusive solutions, including, among others, in the educational and health sectors.[9] In any case, better knowledge of what works and what does not will help policy makers better leverage the potential benefits of stakeholder engagement.

Promoting enabling conditions for stakeholder engagement

Despite challenges, governments can use a number of enabling conditions and policy levers to mainstream inclusive policy making through stakeholder engagement.

These build on lessons learned on open government and digital governance, citizen participation, regulatory policy, budgetary governance, as well as from recent work on water governance.[10]

1. Leverage legal frameworks to encourage and facilitate stakeholder engagement.

In some areas, such as regulatory policy, stakeholder engagement has become part of the policy-making requirements. Albeit an important enabler, legal requirements are neither a sufficient nor an indispensable condition to ensure successful stakeholder engagement.

2. Clarify the objectives of stakeholder engagement, the process of engagement and the scope of stakeholder engagement.

Objectives for, and limits to, engagement should be well defined from the outset, as should the roles and responsibilities of all parties.

3. Identify and reach out to those groups who have a stake in the outcome, including under-represented groups.

Reasonable effort should be made to engage with all relevant stakeholders, including by targeting the "willing but unable" and the "able but unwilling" who hold important situational knowledge. Effort should be made to find the appropriate delivery mechanism to increase the likelihood that their voice be heard.

4. Mainstream stakeholder engagement in the entire policy cycle.

To shape better outcomes, engagement should be mainstreamed throughout the policy process, including: i) identifying policy priorities; ii) drafting the actual policy document; iii) implementing the policy; and iv) evaluating its impacts.

5. Line up institutional resources and delivery tools.

A wide range of tools is increasingly available, including online platforms, social media and open data to broadly engage different segments of the population. At the same time, these tools can be adapted to the user, including by "minding the digital gap".

6. Build effective feedback loops into policy making and with engaged stakeholders,

By using the feedback received to inform decisions and by providing feedback to stakeholders on the use of their inputs.

7. Evaluate the effectiveness of stakeholder engagement.

Systematic evaluation is needed to continuously adapt the tools and approaches to stakeholder engagement, as well as to build a solid business case for engagement, including both the costs and benefits.

8. Keep stakeholder engagement flexible to manage risks and resilient to adapt to changing circumstances.

Stakeholder engagement tools work differently across levels of government, places, times, objectives, stages of the policy cycle, etc. Hence, it is important to tailor engagement mechanisms to each context, types of stakeholders and place-based needs. In addition, as governance systems are dynamic, stakeholder engagement processes should be flexible enough to adapt to changing circumstances.

9. Embed the values of openness and engagement within the administration at all levels of government. Effective stakeholder engagement requires changing the administrative culture.

This involves embedding a culture of inclusion in policy making in the administration from the leadership to the employees, and giving government officials access to appropriate skills, guidance and training.

How inclusive is your workforce? An inclusive workforce results in a more balanced approach to decision making and more engaged front-line staff.

Shaping better outcomes through an inclusive public sector workforce

A diverse, engaged public sector workforce is essential to enable a culture of openness and engagement.

Making inclusion a priority in workforce management sends a clear signal that all groups are welcome to contribute to government and governance. At an operational level, diverse leadership and teams are more likely to find innovative solutions and work across silos when empowered to do so (OECD, 2011a). This is most evident at the senior management level, where evidence shows that inclusion results in a more balanced approach to decision-making and, in the private sector, better bottom-line outcomes. In addition, a core element of a more inclusive public sector workforce is employee engagement. Statistics show that more engaged front line staff appears to provide more satisfying service experiences to the citizens they serve. Evidence also suggests that satisfaction with public service delivery is positively correlated to citizen trust in government and governance.[11]

Work policies that favour work/life balance, promote diversity in leadership functions and encourage a diverse public sector workforce.

Inclusion requires a holistic approach to employee engagement.

Inclusion requires not only a workforce whose diversity reflects the population it serves, but also an organisational culture and a development strategy that enable each and every staff member to contribute their full potential. Complex employee surveys on perception and engagement can be used to identify data- driven strategies, as was done by the German Employment Agency (Box 21). Policy areas that can contribute to an inclusion strategy include reconciling work and life, promoting diversity in leadership functions at all levels, equally sharing family responsibilities, and managing using an intergenerational life-cycle approach with appropriate working conditions, lifelong learning and knowledge management (Gerpott et al, 2015). These approaches can also be encouraged beyond the public sector, as done by the Austrian Government's "work and family audits".[12]

Box 3.12 The life-cycle oriented human resource policy of the German Employment Agency

The life-cycle-oriented human resource policy of the Bundesagentur für Arbeit (BA) in Germany uses an intergenerational approach to enhance the work ability of its staff; the policy focuses on competencies, health and engagement to promote lifelong learning and well-being in the workplace. The intergenerational approach is also embedded in an overall strategy to deliver customer-oriented services effectively and efficiently. With its life cycle-oriented HR policy, the BA pursues a highly flexible strategy that offers the best possible reconciliation of work and private life in comparison with employer interests. As a result, in an internal survey 61% of employees rated their personal reconciliation of work and private life as good or very good. Almost 80% of staff regarded equal opportunity policies as very important. Services and tools in the BA's intergenerational management approach deliberately target employees at the beginning, in the middle as well as at the end of their professional careers and beyond. The BA considers this policy, which includes corporate health management as well as knowledge management, as providing significant leverage to enhance engagement and motivation; these can be correlated with customer satisfaction and individual and organisational performance.

Source: German Employment Agency.

Inclusiveness starts with gender equality. Although women are well represented in the public sector workforce, they sill lag behind in parity in management and leadership positions.

Gender equality is arguably the most universal challenge to public workforce inclusion across OECD countries, despite its well-known positive impact on governance outcomes.

Available data points to lower levels of inequality in countries with a greater share of women in legislatures and shows a positive relationship between women ministers and confidence in national governments (Mavisakalyan, 2012; Rehavi, 2007). While generally well represented in OECD countries' public sector workforce, women they still lag behind in parity in management and leadership positions. Despite variations, women consistently occupy less than half of public service decision-making positions, on average accounting only for 28.6% of senior managers across OECD countries (Figure 3.8). Nonetheless, generational shifts, increasing levels of education and changing perspectives as a result of a new socio-economic reality and sustained efforts towards diversity, are contributing to an increase of the number of women in management positions, although mainly in middle management (OECD, 2014b).

Figure 3.8 Share of central government jobs filled by women, by occupation groups (2010)

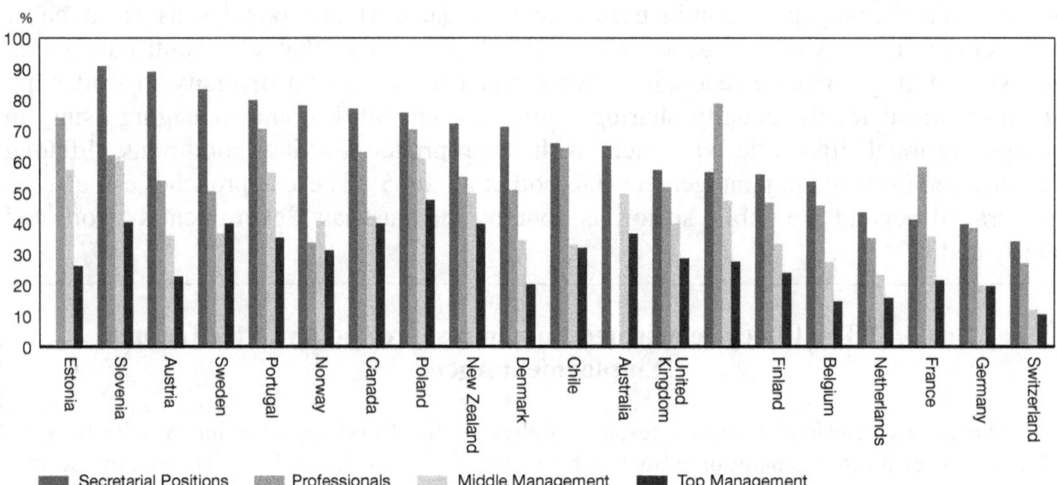

Note: Data for Luxembourg, Slovenia and Sweden are for 2011 rather than 2010. Data for France are for 2009 rather than 2010. Data for the Netherlands are in full-time equivalent. Data for Switzerland on secretarial positions also include technical positions.

Source: OECD (2013b), based on data from OECD (2011).

Equality, diversity and inclusion policies need to be aligned with human resource management and leadership tools to build an inclusive civil service.

Several actions could be implemented to undertake such objectives. Strengthening leadership and enhancing management and executive accountability are fundamental. Being an attractive employer implies competitive salaries, a stable work environment, opportunities for growth and development, constructive social dialog, and a culture that encourages senior managers to "speak truth to power" and provide evidence-based advice without fear of retribution. Inclusion can also be enhanced by improving work-life balance options and promoting flexibility, transparency, and fairness of the public sector employment systems and policies. Finally, monitoring and evaluating diversity and inclusion programmes on a regular basis and holding managers and public employees accountable also constitute essential measures; these are necessary to adjust policies, goals and methods to improve the equality and diversity of the public administration over the long run.

Mainstreaming inclusive policy making for inclusive growth

Together with government-led efforts to consolidate integrity frameworks that help avert the risk of capture in policy making, societies are rapidly evolving towards new forms of engagement of various stakeholders.

Under the paradigm of open government – collaborative governance, open data and co-production, for instance – higher levels of engagement hold promise for inclusive policy making, particularly in the context of inclusive growth. Inclusive policy making, especially through stakeholder engagement, can help shape priorities that closely match the needs of society, including those of underserved or excluded social groups.

Still, challenges to stakeholder engagement in support of inclusive policy making remain.

Stakeholder engagement can be undermined by inadequate representation, inaccessibility of information, obstacles to civic participation and inadequate use of inputs received, among others. Beyond these challenges, there is a need to dispel the myths around stakeholder engagement. Even with the best intentions and the framework conditions in place, stakeholder engagement still risks failing to achieve an inclusive process and may even entail capture if not properly handled. A number of exogenous and endogenous factors may explain failed engagement processes, including the lack of consideration of contexts and place-based specific dimensions.

Policy capture destroys inclusion. While progress is being made, much more needs to be done to defend policy against capture by narrow interests.

Mechanisms designed to prevent the risk of undue access and of influence by powerful, better organised interest groups are needed in tandem.

Together with openness and engagement, solid integrity frameworks for policy making can help ensure that final policy decisions reflect the views of the many, and not just the few. Generally, countries have made progress in establishing the essential remedies to avert policy capture and safeguard inclusive policy making based on increasing transparency and integrity in lobbying, better managing conflict of interest and balancing political finance. Yet, more work needs to be done as some exiting practices and legislative loopholes (e.g. third party funding in political finance) still remain vulnerable to exploitation by powerful narrow interests.

Digital government, including open government data (OGD) and social media, has a growing role to play in stakeholder engagement and collaboration.

Continued efforts should be made to collect evidence on successful engagement practices and impacts to ensure that stakeholder engagement meets its promises and adapts to technological changes.

In particular, there is a need to deepen the understanding of the contribution of stakeholder engagement to inclusive policy making, its drivers and policy enablers. The ongoing OECD data collection on open government and citizen participation in the policy cycle will help to identify common trends and challenges and provide evidence for better stakeholder engagement for inclusive growth. Digital government, including open government data and social media, can be further leveraged as enablers of new and innovative forms of engagement and collaboration. Through this, the OECD will also contribute to collecting evidence on the impact of stakeholder engagement in better policy outcomes.

Greater guidance and practical toolkits should be provided to governments on how engagement practices can be further embedded in policy making.

In particular, further guidance building from successful and less successful practices should be provided in the areas of budgeting and rule-making as they are the critical tools of policy making and essential levers of welfare and redistribution. In particular, much remains to be done in terms of providing practical guidance for engagement regarding targeting various segments of the population, the length of the engagement process and its sequence, and efficient ways of acknowledging feedback and taking it into account. Much can also be learned from the applied knowledge of stakeholder engagement in specific sectors, in particular water where engagement practices have developed at all levels of government.

Looking forward, the OECD will continue deepening the understanding, evidence and guidance on inclusive institutions and their role in shaping inclusive growth outcomes.

Enabling conditions for shaping inclusive policies, including by ensuring inclusion in the public sector workforce should also be a priority. Further work on diversity, inclusion and employee engagement through collecting indicators related to these areas, as well as through research on leadership and public employment policies, will help countries define comprehensive strategies to attract and retain the best talent in the public sector. It will also build more inclusive institutions, more inclusive societies and more inclusive growth.

Notes

1 See www.gov.uk/service-manual/digital-by-default.

2 For example, Traber (2013) finds that "public interest groups report higher satisfaction with the policy outcome, the more they participate". Essaiason et al. (2012) find that "personal involvement is the main factor generating legitimacy beliefs".

3 Elinor Ostrom (2010) demonstrates that solidarity-based economies are promising alternatives to state-centred command-and-control economic solutions to pressing social and ecological problems.

4 Findings of the 6th OECD Expert Meeting on Measuring Regulatory Performance www.oecd.org/gov/regulatory-policy/the-hague-workshop.htm.

5 Subnational governments across the OECD manage 40% of public expenditure, 50% of public procurement, 59% of public investment and 63% of public sector staff expenditure (OECD, 2014c).

6 See www.telegraph.co.uk/education/educationnews/9334721/Neverseconds-Martha-Payne-the-unsquashable-school-meal-crusader-aged-nine.html.

7 For a more in-depth discussion on youth and public governance see OECD, 2016; OECD, 2015h and OECD 2015i.

8 For an overview of the evaluation of efforts of digital engagement in the United States from a US perspective, see Evans and Campos, 2013.

9 For cases and examples, see OECD, 2011b.

10 Including the Guiding Principles on Open and Inclusive Policymaking, the Best Practice Principles on regulatory Policy: Stakeholder Engagement, the Checklist on Stakeholder Engagement for Inclusive Water Governance, the Recommendation on Digital Government Strategies and the forthcoming Recommendation on Gender Equality in Public Life.

11 National Human Services Assembly, NYU Wagner School of Public Service, Capstone Consulting Project, Developing Senior Management Diversity, Spring 2011.

12 For an overview of the correlations between public servants commitment, satisfaction with public service delivery and citizen trust in government, see Heintzman and Marson, 2005.

References

Alemanno, A. (2015), "Stakeholder engagement in regulatory policy", OECD Working Paper, OECD Publishing, Paris.

Allan (2014), Findings of the 6th OECD Expert Meeting on Measuring Regulatory Performance, www.oecd.org/gov/regulatory-policy/the-hague-workshop.htm.

DHSSPS (2002), Investing for Health, Department of Health, Social Services and Public Safety, www.dhsspsni.gov.uk/invest1.pdf.

Esaiasson et al. (2012). Which decision-making arrangements generate the strongest legitimacy beliefs? Evidence from a randomised field experiment. European Journal of Political Research Volume 51, Issue 6, pages 785–808, October 2012.

Etzioni (2009), *Minorities and the National Ethos*, Politics Volume 29, Issue 2, pages 100–110, June 2009.

Evans, A. and A. Campos (2013), "Open government initiatives: Challenges of citizen participation", Journal of Policy Analyses and Management, 32(1), pp. 178-179.

Fernandez Guerra, C. (2014), @polic.a: las historias de un .xito, Aguilar Press, Madrid.

Fries, S., T. Lysenko and S. Polanec (2003), The 2002 Business Environment and Enterprise Performance Survey: Results from a Survey of 6,100 Firms, London.

Gerpott, R. et al (2015) Age-Diverse Training Groups: How Knowledge Sharing & Psychological Safety Promote Learning Outcomes, Academy of Management Proceedings 2015 (1), 11691, http://proceedings.aom.org/content/2015/1/11691.short

Heintzman, R. and B. Marson (2005), "People, service and trust: Is there a public sector service value chain?", International Review of Administrative Sciences 4/2005 (Vol. 71), pp. 583-612.

Hellman, J. S., G. Jones and D. Kaufmann (2003), "Seize the state, seize the day: State capture and influence in transition economies", Journal of Comparative Economics 31(4), pp. 751-773.

Mairie de Paris (2015), Budget participatif, https://budgetparticipatif.paris.fr/bp/le-budget-participatif-.html.

Mavisakalyan, A. (2012), "Women in cabinet and public health spending: Evidence across countries", ANU Working Papers no. 574, Australian National University.

McLean, I. and A. McMillan (eds.) (2009), The Concise Oxford Dictionary of Politics, Oxford University Press, Oxford.

Mickoleit, A. (2014), "Social media use by governments: A policy primer to discuss trends, identify policy opportunities and guide decision makers", OECD Working Papers on Public Governance, No. 26, OECD Publishing, Paris, http://dx.doi.org/10.1787/5jxrcmghmk0s-en.

OECD (forthcoming 2016), Safeguarding Inclusive Public Decision-Making by Curbing the Risks of Policy Capture, OECD, Paris.

OECD (2016) *Open Government Review of Tunisia*, OECD Public Governance Reviews, OECD Publishing, Paris, http://www.keepeek.com/Digital-Asset-Management/oecd/governance/open-government-in-tunisia_9789264227118-en#page1

OECD (2015a), *Stakeholder Engagement for Inclusive Water Governance*, OECD Studies on Water, OECD Publishing, Paris, http://dx.doi.org/10.1787/9789264231122-en.

OECD (2015b), *OECD Regulatory Policy Outlook 2015*, OECD Publishing, Paris, http://dx.doi.org/10.1787/9789264238770-en.

OECD (2015c), *Lithuania: Fostering Open and Inclusive Policy Making*, OECD Public Governance Reviews, OECD Publishing, Paris, http://dx.doi.org/10.1787/9789264235762-en.

OECD (2015d), "OECD Recommendation of the Council on Budgetary Governance", [C (2015) 1], OECD, Paris.

OECD (2015e), *Stakeholder Engagement for Inclusive Water Governance*, OECD Studies on Water, OECD Publishing, Paris, http://dx.doi.org/10.1787/9789264231122-en.

OECD (2015f), *Open Government Data Review of Poland: Unlocking the Value of Government Data*, OECD Digital Government Studies, OECD Publishing, Paris, http://dx.doi.org/10.1787/9789264241787-en

OECD (2015g), *Government at a Glance 2015*, OECD Publishing, Paris, http://dx.doi.org/10.1787/gov_glance-2015-en.

OECD (2015h) "Public governance frameworks for Open Government in Morocco", in *Open Government in Morocco*, OECD Publishing, Paris, http://dx.doi.org/10.1787/9789264226685-6-en

OECD (2015i), *All on Board: Making Inclusive Growth Happen*, OECD Publishing, Paris, http://dx.doi.org/10.1787/9789264218512-en.

OECD (2014a), *Open Government in Latin America*, OECD Public Governance Reviews, OECD Publishing, Paris, http://dx.doi.org/10.1787/9789264223639-en

OECD (2014a), *Open Government in Latin America*, OECD Public Governance Reviews, OECD Publishing, Paris, http://dx.doi.org/10.1787/9789264223639-en

OECD (2014b), *Women, Government and Policy Making in OECD Countries: Fostering Diversity for Inclusive Growth*, OECD Publishing, Paris, http://dx.doi.org/10.1787/9789264210745-en.

OECD (2013a), Investing in Trust: Leveraging Institutions for Inclusive Policymaking, OECD, Paris, http://www.oecd.org/gov/ethics/Investing-in-trust.pdf.

OECD (2013b), *Government at a Glance 2013*, OECD Publishing, Paris, http://dx.doi.org/10.1787/gov_glance-2013-en.

OECD (2012), *OECD Reviews of Regional Innovation: Central and Southern Denmark 2012*, OECD Reviews of Regional Innovation, OECD Publishing, Paris, http://dx.doi.org/10.1787/9789264178748-en.

OECD (2011a), *Public Servants as Partners for Growth: Toward a Stronger, Leaner and More Equitable Workforce*, OECD Publishing, Paris, http://dx.doi.org/10.1787/9789264166707-en.

OECD (2011b), *Together for Better Public Services: Partnering with Citizens and Civil Society*, OECD Public Governance Reviews, OECD Publishing, Paris, http://dx.doi.org/10.1787/9789264118843-en.

OECD (2009), *Focus on Citizens: Public Engagement for Better Policy and Services*, OECD Studies on Public Engagement, OECD Publishing, Paris, http://dx.doi.org/10.1787/9789264048874-en.

OECD (2005), *Modernising Government: The Way Forward*, OECD Publishing, Paris, http://dx.doi.org/10.1787/9789264010505-en.

OECD (2001), *Citizens as Partners: OECD Handbook on Information, Consultation and Public Participation in Policy-Making*, OECD Publishing, Paris, http://dx.doi.org/10.1787/9789264195578-en.

Ostrom, E. (2010), *Beyond markets and states: Polycentric governance of complex economic systems*, American Economic Review, Vol. 100, Issue 3, pp. 641-672, http://dx.doi.org/10.1257/aer.100.3.641.

Rehavi, M. (2007), "Sex and politics: Do female legislators affect state spending?", University of California, Berkeley.

Thomas, C. et al. (2010), "Special Interest Capture of Regulatory Agencies: A Ten-Year Analysis of Voting Behaviour on Regional Fishery Management Councils", The Policy Studies Journal, Vol. 38, No. 3, pp. 447-464.

Traber, D. (2013), "Does participation in policymaking enhance satisfaction with the policy outcome? Evidence from Switzerland", Swiss Political Science Review, 19, pp. 60-83.

Warren, M. E. (2003), "What does corruption mean in a democracy", American Journal of Political Science, 48(2), pp. 328-343.

ORGANISATION FOR ECONOMIC CO-OPERATION AND DEVELOPMENT

The OECD is a unique forum where governments work together to address the economic, social and environmental challenges of globalisation. The OECD is also at the forefront of efforts to understand and to help governments respond to new developments and concerns, such as corporate governance, the information economy and the challenges of an ageing population. The Organisation provides a setting where governments can compare policy experiences, seek answers to common problems, identify good practice and work to co-ordinate domestic and international policies.

The OECD member countries are: Australia, Austria, Belgium, Canada, Chile, the Czech Republic, Denmark, Estonia, Finland, France, Germany, Greece, Hungary, Iceland, Ireland, Israel, Italy, Japan, Korea, Luxembourg, Mexico, the Netherlands, New Zealand, Norway, Poland, Portugal, the Slovak Republic, Slovenia, Spain, Sweden, Switzerland, Turkey, the United Kingdom and the United States. The European Union takes part in the work of the OECD.

OECD Publishing disseminates widely the results of the Organisation's statistics gathering and research on economic, social and environmental issues, as well as the conventions, guidelines and standards agreed by its members.

OECD PUBLISHING, 2, rue André-Pascal, 75775 PARIS CEDEX 16
(42 2016 19 1 P) ISBN 978-92-64-25798-6 – 2016

www.ingramcontent.com/pod-product-compliance
Lightning Source LLC
LaVergne TN
LVHW081418110826
845149LV00010B/1786

* 9 7 8 9 2 6 4 2 5 7 9 8 6 *

Graphique 1.32. **Variation de la production de déchets municipaux par habitant depuis 2000**

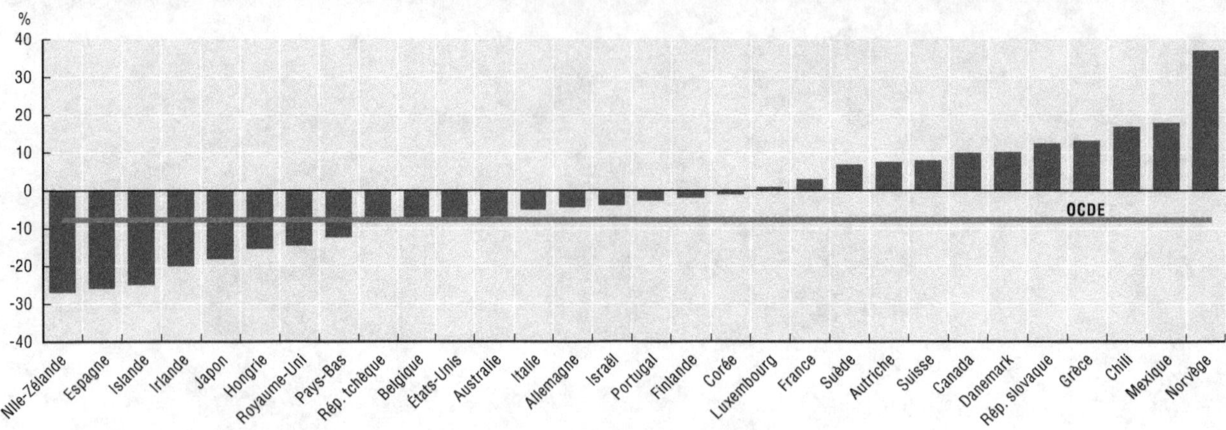

Source : OCDE (2015), « Déchets municipaux », *Statistiques de l'OCDE sur l'environnement* (base de données).

StatLink http://dx.doi.org/10.1787/888933365194

Graphique 1.33. **Variation de la quantité de déchets municipaux mise en décharge par habitant depuis 2000**

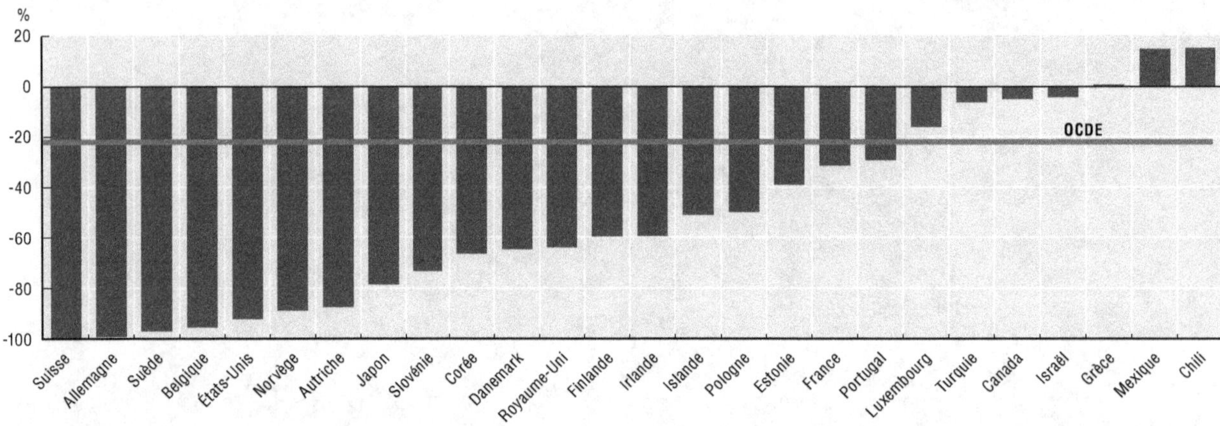

Source : OCDE (2015), « Déchets municipaux », *Statistiques de l'OCDE sur l'environnement* (base de données).

StatLink http://dx.doi.org/10.1787/888933365207

Graphique 1.34. **Variation de la quantité de déchets municipaux valorisée par habitant depuis 2000**

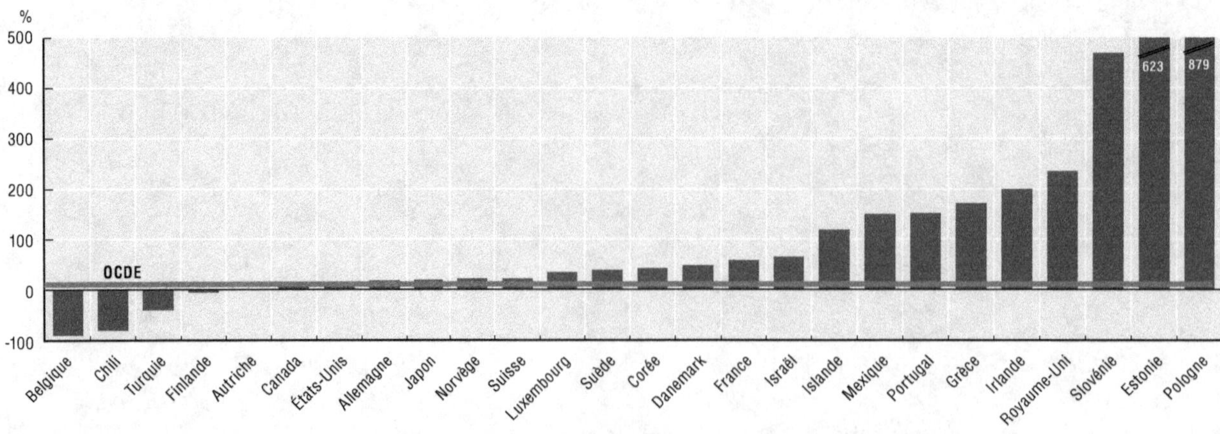

Source : OCDE (2015), « Déchets municipaux », *Statistiques de l'OCDE sur l'environnement* (base de données).

StatLink http://dx.doi.org/10.1787/888933365213